DATE DUE			
Feb 28'72			

THE GREAT DREADNOUGHT

BOOKS BY RICHARD HOUGH

THE GREAT DREADNOUGHT

The Strange Story of H. M. S. Agincourt,
The Mightiest Battleship of
World War I

RICHARD HOUGH

Harper & Row, Publishers, New York and Evanston

940.45942
H81g
7 7760
Feb.1972

Most of the contents of this book appeared originally in *The New Yorker,* in slightly different form.

FIRST U.S. EDITION

LIBRARY OF CONGRESS CATALOG CARD NUMBER: 66-21709

To all who served in "The Gin Palace"

ACKNOWLEDGEMENTS

I have had an unusual amount of personal help in gathering information and checking facts for this book. No one has given more of his time (and hospitality) than Admiral Sir Angus Cunninghame Graham, K.B.E., C.B., who read the manuscript at three stages after a long and intensive questioning, and also provided several unique photographs from his personal diaries. Admiral Frank Elliott, O.B.E., was also most helpful, especially on his experiences with the training of Turkish recruits in 1914, and also provided me with several photographs. Vice-Admiral Jack Egerton, C.B., another ex-officer from the *Agincourt* gave me additional material which was most useful. Among foreign naval officers who were liberal in their co-operation and helped me with checking facts and providing illustrations were Captain F. Kent Loomis, the Acting Director of Naval History in Washington, Captain Rashit Metel of the Turkish Navy, and Capitao-de-Fragata Alfredo Vasconellos Cunha of the Brazilian Navy. Lieutenant-Commander P. K. Kemp, O.B.E., and David Woodward were kind enough to read my manuscript and correct me on several points; and Mr. W. Tynemouth F.L.A., the City Librarian of Newcastle upon Tyne City Libraries and Mr. B. Collingwood Stevenson, Director of the Laing Art Gallery and the Museum of Science and Engineering at Newcastle upon Tyne, were especially helpful during my visits to their city. Among a great number of people who worked on the ship when she was being built on Tyneside and who suffered patiently my interrogations, I must name Messrs. C. G. Piaff, Peter Gibbons, James C. Bell, J. G. Gray and J. R. Gray, G. C. Smith and Stan Johnston. Mr. W. P. Trotter kindly loaned me several unique photographs, and I am indebted to the Imperial War Museum for two of the photographs of the *Agincourt* at sea during the First World War. Messrs. Hutchinson and Co. Ltd., kindly allowed me to quote from *A Shipbuilder's Yarn: the Record of a Naval Constructor* by Sir Eustace H. W. Tennyson d'Eyncourt, Bt.

CONTENTS

THE GREAT DREADNOUGHT

CHAPTER ONE

The Good Salesman

In the golden age of the big battleship before the first of
the great wars, when this weapon represented in all its
magnificence a nation's ranking in the power stakes, warship
salesmen of many nations travelled the world in search of
orders. These were no ordinary salesmen with a bag of samples
and a well-rehearsed patter. If the present world allowed such
things, these men today would be peddling I.C.B.M.s or
nuclear submarines to the new African states, or perhaps to
China. Success in securing the order for a single battleship
could mean a contract for some two-and-a-half million pounds
(around £18m in modern money) and employment for
several thousand men for two or three years. These were
salesmen on the grandest scale, often supported directly or
indirectly by the treasuries and foreign offices of the great
shipbuilding powers. Wherever they travelled their embassies
and consulates and export agencies and banks encouraged and
sustained them in their efforts to seal contracts. It sometimes
happened that political pressure was resorted to in an effort to
clinch a deal.

Most of these important warship salesmen led a delegation
of technical experts and advisers, who brought with them
scale models, portfolios of blueprints and drawings of proposed designs. Sometimes they settled in ostentatious mansions
and spent lavishly on hospitality. The great arms company of
Krupp possessed a permanent residence of great grandeur
outside Constantinople. One French company spent £25,000

in an unsuccessful attempt to acquire a contract for two South American battleships. The United States Navy despatched its best Dreadnought battleship to Valparaiso, where it remained off-shore, mighty and intimidating, while delegates of the Fore River Shipyard entered into negotiations with the Chilean Minister of Marine and his senior officers for the construction of two battleships. They, too, failed.

In the two decades before 1914 these sales missions from the leading shipyards—among them Krupps and Blohm and Voss from Germany, New York Shipbuilding and Fore River from the United States, Vickers—Maxim and Armstrong Whitworth from Britain, and the leading companies from France and Italy—hurried to any nation at the first hint that it had become infected by the Dreadnought fever that was sweeping the world. Not all of them competed for the richest prizes. La Seyne of France built cruisers for Spain, Cramps of Philadelphia a protected cruiser for Turkey, Schichau of Elbing destroyers for Russia and Roumania, the Italian companies of Orlando and Ansaldo constructed cruisers for the Portuguese and Argentine navies. Krupps of course were active everywhere, and among the orders secured by one British yard were cruisers for Mexico and Peru, and battleships for Turkey, Chile and Japan. But the greatest of them all, an exporter extraordinary of guns and shells as well as warships, was the company of Sir W. G. Armstrong, Whitworth and Co. Ltd., whose massive ordnance works, shell shops and slipways lined the northern banks of the river at Newcastle upon Tyne in Northumberland. Armstrongs was almost synonymous with Newcastle, employing some 30,000 men, when times were good. Their gun-shops and shipyards extended from Scotswood down river through Elswick to Walker. The prosperity of this chill, dark city rose and fell with international anxiety. A peace conference spelt depression; a rash of South American jingoism, a spot of trouble in the Balkans, could put colour in the cheeks of the children playing between the workmen's dwellings of Westmorland Road and Bell Terrace. Armstrongs was the most successful exporter of warships in the world, and they held this position by reason of the quality both of their products and their sales organization.

In 1904 Armstrongs made one of their shrewdest appointments. Eustace Hugh Tennyson d'Eyncourt possessed in the highest degree all the qualifications required for supervising the design, promotion and sale of Armstrong's warships abroad. His background and connections were impeccable, his appearance, marked by a light frame, commanding height, a fine narrow face and aristocratic features, properly matched the expectations of foreign purchasing commissions and ministers of marine, and was calculated to inspire confidence in his integrity and authority. One of his uncles was an admiral in the Royal Navy, and he was a cousin of the late Poet Laureate, Alfred, Lord Tennyson. Ships had fascinated Tennyson d'Eyncourt since early childhood, when he used to make models and sail them on the lake of the family estate at Hadley House in Hertfordshire. After completing his education at Charterhouse, introductions to the late Chief Constructor of the Navy and no less a person than the Director of Naval Construction, Sir William White, ensured young Tennyson d'Eyncourt's nomination to an apprenticeship with Armstrongs. He served this in full through six arduous years, through frame bending, riveting—at the furnaces, at the blacksmiths' and carpenters' shops, working always closely with the workmen who were later to build the battleships he designed. This was followed by a course in naval architecture at the Royal Naval College at Greenwich, a further term in the designs department at Elswick, and a period with a Clydeside shipbuilding firm before returning to Armstrongs in 1902. Two years later he was sent out on the Orient Express to Constantinople to supervise the handing over to the Turkish government of three ships Armstrongs had built for the Turkish government—including a "lavish and luxurious" yacht for the Sultan, and "an equally gorgeous" state barge for ceremonial occasions, as he described them—and to persuade the Sultan and the Ministry of Marine to order more warships from Armstrongs. Tennyson d'Eyncourt conducted this first overseas assignment with such success that he was invited by the Turks to remain in order to carry out a complete survey of the navy, for which he was awarded a suitable decoration in spite of the fact that he found the fleet in a deplorable state of neglect.

This was the first of many arduous missions to foreign navies in the dual role of designer and salesman. France, Italy, Greece, Turkey, China and Japan, Spain and South American republics were among the countries he visited, and the results were gratifying for Armstrongs. In contrast with his rivals, he travelled alone with his wife, avoiding the ostentatious front put up by some of the German, French and Italian sales delegations, preferring to rely on his wide technical knowledge and the unique reputation of Armstrongs. It was a style and policy that rarely failed. On technical grounds alone it was difficult to resist his persuasion. His love for great warships which he had possessed since childhood was supported by an outstanding skill as a designer.

During his term of office with Armstrongs, this remarkable designer-salesman became deeply involved in the sad and curious business of South American arms rivalry, which was to lead to a race to build the biggest battleship in the world. Among the republics, Brazil was the most fervently belligerent, most bellicose in its demeanour, most hell-bent on Armageddon. The reasons for this are no more explicable now than they were at the time, although the full-blooded and emotional temperament of the people played its full part. Brazil had no designs on her neighbours and was not threatened by them. Certainly neither Brazil nor any of the other South American republics could afford to construct or maintain the outsize fleets that year by year further strained their resources and swelled their inadequate dockyards and bases. The country's relations with both Chile and the Argentine could hardly have been more cordial. Frontier disputes, which in the past had sometimes flamed into minor wars, had been settled by arbitration, and even the vexed question of the ownership of the Misiones territory had been resolved through the good offices of the American president, Grover Cleveland, as long before as 1895. And yet for more than a decade the larger South American powers had become increasingly involved in a competition of maritime power which had no apparent purpose nor meaning. Even the humblest, most poverty stricken republic had determined to make some sort of claim to status by purchasing at least one or two obsolete and unwanted men-of-war from America or the European naval powers. This expensive practice certainly allowed those in power to enjoy a degree of self-esteem, and the contemplation of these vessels from time to time offered the common people some self-satisfaction and even a sense of security. But the only direct beneficiaries were the workers and shareholders of the large foreign armament companies, especially those of Britain.

South American naval rivalry had begun at the turn of the century, when new fire was added to German-British competition by Admiral Alfred von Tirpitz's Navy Bill of 1900, and continued for the next twelve years in an imitative tempo. It seemed that each republic, without cause or thought, was impelled to further excesses by the examples of Britain and Germany, America and Japan, and the other wealthier powers who year by year appropriated more money for the construction of mighty Dreadnoughts. The Chileans were the first off the mark, in 1901. They were at that time in a vulnerable condition, being engaged in a somewhat critical frontier dispute with the Argentine, whose naval strength was greatly superior to their own. The British naval architect, Sir Edward Reed, happened conveniently to be in the Chilean capital at that time, and was able to satisfy the Chilean Admiral Moutt that Armstrongs was well able to meet the navy's urgent requirements. Two fast battleships, the *Constitution* and *Libertad*, were at once ordered. Later, a growing awareness of their huge cost—almost two million pounds —coincided with a diminution in the crisis, and the Chilean government were happy to have them taken off their hands by the Royal Navy. But the laying down of the keels of these vessels provided the first impetus to the cycle of make-believe fear that revolved ever faster over the following years, as if in an effort to match the pace of the European drive towards Nemesis. During the crisis the Argentine had also ordered from Europe fast armoured cruisers, and as a result the Brazilian government suddenly became conscious of a sense of inferiority inappropriate to a nation with a coastline far longer than her neighbours', and an area larger than that of the United States. While relations remained as amiable as ever, a policy of self-assertion seemed to be demanded by the new circumstances, and the Brazilians decided that a rearmament programme should be carried out on a scale that even the Argentine would be unable to match. On December 14th, 1904, the Brazilian Congress authorized the President to put in hand the construction of no less than twenty-nine warships, including three battleships, three armoured cruisers, six destroyers, twelve torpedo boats and some submarines: a fleet that would at once promote the nation to the position of a considerable world naval power, and an omnipotent South American power. The battleships, the ultimate Edwardian deterrents, were to be put in hand first, but before negotiations were concluded with Armstrongs, rumours of a revolutionary warship being prepared for the Royal Navy began to be heard, and Tennyson d'Eyncourt advised the Brazilian Ministry of Marine to suspend their plans until details became known. In fact the British committee on designs, which was to be responsible for H.M.S. *Dreadnought,* met for the first time a week after the Brazilian Congress's decision was taken, and this first "all-big-gun" ship which at once made obsolete every other battleship in the world, took to the water at Portsmouth little more than a year later. By good fortune and the enthusiastic co-operation of her British suppliers, Brazil thus found herself at the head of the hastily-formed international queue for Dreadnoughts. Armstrongs drew up a new design which showed many improvements on the *Dreadnought* herself. The first of these battleships was

laid down at Armstrong's Elswick yard on the Tyne early
in 1907, the second at Barrow by Vickers Sons and Maxim
Ltd. a few months later, while a decision on the third was
postponed until Brazil's neighbours revealed their counter-
plans. Brazil therefore found herself in 1910 possessed of two
of the most powerful Dreadnoughts in the world, before
Japan or any of the European naval powers except Britain
had taken delivery of their first all-big-gun ships.

These splendid vessels, the *Minas Geraes* and *Sao Paulo,*
were to serve in two world wars and a number of mutinies,
disturbances and revolutions. But long before their arrival in
South American waters steps were being taken by Brazil's
neighbours to anticipate the menace of their presence and
readjust the balance of maritime power. The Argentine began
modestly enough with orders from Armstrongs for a pair of
1,000-ton gunboats. But following the visit of a naval commission to Europe to study warship construction and developments, the Argentine Chamber of Congress in December 1908
passed by a majority of 49 to 13 a bill authorizing the expenditure of eleven million pounds on armaments, including two
battleships. "It was not to be expected," wrote Lord Brassey
in his *Naval Annual,* "that the Argentine Republic would
allow Brazil's naval programme to remain unanswered, and
it is stated that if Brazil continues to increase her fleet, a third
battleship will be laid down."

At this time the anxiety in Britain about German battleship
output had signalled the opening of a campaign, of which
the catch couplet, spread by the press and heard even in the
streets, ran: "We want eight! / And we won't wait!" By
these standards, the South American Dreadnought race still
appeared numerically trivial, but the cost of the Argentine's
two battleships represented almost a fifth of her total annual
revenue. Similar jargon was heard in South America as in
Britain and Germany. Launching speeches provided excellent jingoistic opportunity. "Some people have declared that
Brazil has no need of such mighty battleships for her protection," declared a Brazilian admiral after another of his

country's Dreadnoughts had taken to the water. "We are not constructing a large fleet as a luxury or a pageant." In the Argentine press and among big-navy advocates, the term most often used was "equilibrium of armaments" with the country's northern neighbour. In contrast with the British public, the common people of Brazil and the Argentine responded in a mainly temperate manner to the campaigns of the pressure groups. There were some minor demonstrations, and in August 1910, at a time when Brazil was taking delivery of her first two Dreadnoughts, the flag of the Brazilian Consulate in Buenos Aires was outraged. The government, however, hastened to lament this act, and declared that relations with Brazil remained undisturbed. The correspondent of *The Times* even suggested that "taxpayers in both countries are inclined to support the somewhat daring proposition from Buenos Aires that Brazil should keep the first Dreadnought, cede the second to Argentina, and cancel the order for the third."

But nothing of this nature occurred. Whatever the common people might think, the pride of the Argentine government was deeply wounded by the threatened presence in Brazilian waters of two modern battleships, and alarmed by continuing reports that the third battleship was to be even larger than the *Minas Geraes* and *Sao Paulo*. There were even suggestions that it was to be the *ultima Thule* in battleships, of double the tonnage of the first Dreadnoughts that the United States Navy had recently commissioned.

With their acute ear for the sound of distant drums, Armstrongs heard informally about the Argentine's plans to counter Brazilian naval rearmament long before any formal announcement had been made in Buenos Aires. Rumour had it that the two battleships would each be more powerful than the *Minas Geraes*, itself due to be launched by Armstrongs in September. Tennyson d'Eyncourt at once hurried out to Buenos Aires, determined as always to be first on the spot.

Informal discussions with the Minister of Marine were opened at once but Tennyson d'Eyncourt soon realized that he was up against an adversary instead of the ally he had always found at the Brazilian Ministry of Marine. Armstrongs had not built a warship for the Argentine for twenty years. In spite of every effort contracts had been placed again and again with Italian shipyards, Armstrongs having to be content with supplying the guns for some of them. Tennyson d'Eyncourt discovered that there was a curious and disturbing reluctance in Buenos Aires to place the order with the British yard that was already hard at work on their proposed Dreadnoughts' future antagonists.

There were hints that Armstrong's prices were unduly high, that the armoured cruisers Orlando of Italy had constructed for them were highly satisfactory, that the Americans seemed very eager for heavy warship building work these days. "It was," commented Tennyson d'Eyncourt, "a difficult mission." However, he persevered for some three months, and then came home to consult with Armstrong's board. Was it, in fact, worth fighting on?

By this time the whole world knew the massive extent of the Argentine's counter arms programme. The announcement caused no surprise. Nor was it surprising—for the profits could be very considerable—that every shipyard capable of building battleships was now making approaches to the Ministry of Marine in Buenos Aires. These overtures were warmly welcomed by the Argentine, which began to play an extraordinary game of cat-and-mouse with no less than twenty shipbuilding companies from the United States, Britain, France, Germany and Italy. No sooner had the shipyards prepared detailed plans and prices to meet one specification, than the Ministry, still in a state of uncertainty about the size and power of the third Brazilian battleship, changed their specification and invited further tenders. This was an expensive and exhausting business, for it could take many weeks and ten thousand pounds to prepare plans and prices for a Dreadnought. As the bidding became more competitive, pressure

was brought to bear on the Argentine in the form of trade
contracts favourable to the republic, which added to the
evident enjoyment of the clients. The American State Department through the Secretary of State, Mr. Knox, and the
Italian government, were especially active; while the British
Foreign Office, to the exasperation of Tennyson d'Eyncourt,
acted with customary aloofness from common business. The
French threatened to withdraw from the competition. "The
French, German and British shipbuilders who have already
been asked three times for their detailed plans generally com-
plain," ran an editorial in *Moniteur de la Flotte* in December
1909. "It would appear that the secret is not sufficiently kept
as to the successive proposals by the French and foreign
builders. It is even maintained that competitors have got
knowledge thereof, and the interested parties regret this, more
especially as the order seems to have been reserved for Italy.
Now the Argentine Commission asks for a fourth project
from each constructor." Already some one hundred thousand
pounds had been spent on earlier plans.

Armstrongs continued to persevere, however, drew up a
fourth set of drawings, and in December 1909 Tennyson
d'Eyncourt sailed with his wife once again to Buenos Aires.
The American State Department had meanwhile determined
to make what today would be called "loss leaders" of these
two Dreadnoughts. The big east coast shipbuilders were des-
perate for work, and the Bethlehem Steel Company, which
had recently installed expensive capital equipment, needed
the armour plate order so badly that they were prepared to
cut their prices to the bone. In command of the American
sales drive that was to break the British monopoly was Rear-
Admiral Francis T. Bowles of the Fore River Company of
Quincey, Mass. Acting with Secretary Knox, and through
the Latin-American Bureau, and quoting at the last minute
an unprofitable figure of £4,400,000 for the two ships, the
Americans secured the order just when Tennyson d'Eyncourt
thought he was close to success.

It was a severe, and even humiliating blow to this successful salesman-designer. But the journey was to have worse consequences for him. In the midsummer heat of the Argentine capital his wife contracted a serious illness, and a week later she died in the hotel in Buenos Aires where they were staying. "It is impossible to describe how intensely miserable the journey home was for me, a voyage of over a fortnight, and bringing with me in the ship my wife's body for burial at home." Back in England, a month after his wife's funeral, the Americans who had pulled off the coup held a dinner at the Savoy Hotel in London. The host was Admiral Bowles and among the guests were Knox, Archibald Johnston of the Bethlehem Steel Company and the senior officers of the Argentine Naval Commission. It was all very decorously conducted, but for this celebration to take place in the heart of London, at this time and under these circumstances, looked very much like a deliberate affront to Tennyson d'Eyncourt and to Armstrongs.

In less than three years, according to the very tight schedule of construction on which the Argentine navy had insisted, Argentina would be in possession of two Dreadnoughts which would more than offset Brazil's new naval power. At this melancholy period in his life Tennyson d'Eyncourt was glad to immerse himself in his work, and he even looked forward with a special relish to discussing with his friends in Rio de Janeiro the size and gunpower of Brazil's third battleship. A South American arms race on an unprecedented scale was now well into its stride, and good fighting salesman that he was, Tennyson d'Eyncourt was determined not to be out-pointed again.

Meanwhile, in the face of the formidable rearmament programme of the two largest South American republics, Chile changed her mind about battleships, and repented of her earlier decision to sell off the *Constitution* and *Libertad*. As early as February 1906 the German magazine *Marine Rundscau* was reporting that the Chilean government had determined to order a battleship, two cruisers and four destroyers. There was a delay of several years while the specification of

the battleship was discussed and revised, and means of paying for it were investigated, but by 1911 when Brazil was in
possession of her first two Dreadnoughts and the Argentine
was seeking means to stabilize the situation by instituting an
even larger programme than Brazil's, Lord Brassey reported
that "the craze for the construction of monster battleships
which has pervaded South America during the last few years
has now reached Chile." The Chilean Ministry of Marine had
persuaded the government that two Dreadnoughts rather
than one were now necessary to retain the balance of maritime
power, and that it was essential that they should be larger and
more powerful than either Brazil's or Argentina's. Once
again there was a fierce struggle for these valuable contracts,
and as in Buenos Aires, the final contenders in the running
were Armstrongs and American shipyards. This time there
was no failure, and Armstrongs clinched the deal for
both.

The epidemic then spread rapidly. The lesser republics
weighed in. The Uruguayan Minister of Marine General
Eduardo Vasquez ordered a cruiser from Germany, Peru
persuaded the French government to sell off an old 6,000-ton
armoured cruiser to add to the new 6-inch-gunned cruisers
recently built for her in Britain, Venezuela hastily bought a
gunboat, captured by the United States Navy from the
Spanish at Manila, and Ecuador bought an old torpedo boat.
In the course of four busy years every South American state
increased its naval strength many times over, although some
disasters caused by naval inexperience offset these gains.
Uruguay lost a cruiser on the coast of the Rio Grande when
it was on its way to the Brazilian republic's anniversary celebrations, and Chilean sailors salvaged only the guns from
the cruiser *Presidente Pinto* when she ran aground near Tal-
cahuano. Brazil suffered her most severe catastrophe on
January 21st, 1905, during the course of a voyage by three of
her most powerful warships to survey a new military port and
dockyard in Jacarepagua Bay near Angrados Reis. The
powder magazine of the turret ship *Aquidaban* blew up,

causing the deaths of two hundred and twenty-three officers and men, including three rear-admirals. There were numerous miscalculations and minor disasters during this period which pointed to the fact that the demands of rapid naval expansion could be heavy in lives as well as money.

The scale of South American naval rearmament brought other unforeseen hazards in its train besides errors of navigation and seamanship. Naval strength was not only expensive; it was double-edged, and provided revolutionary elements with mobile and powerful weapons. It was also readily corruptible, because rapid expansion had reduced the quality of the personnel, and poor conditions and uncertain pay converted many a bluejacket to an insurrectionary cause. The Brazilian navy, besides suffering the most grievous mishaps, already possessed a reputation for restlessness, dating from the previous decade, when the fleet had provided the most sustained and dangerous opposition to the policies of the new President Floriano Peixoto, and had bombarded Rio de Janeiro with grievous loss of life. In the years between the Peixoto rebellion and the arrival in home waters of her first new Dreadnoughts, the Brazilian fleet suffered only minor outbreaks of mutiny and insubordination and her misfortunes were mainly limited to mishaps. By the end of 1909 the Brazilian naval rearmament programme was approaching its zenith, although the size and specification for the third and biggest battleship had still to be decided. In a message to Congress just before Christmas Vice-Admiral Alexandrino Faria de Alencar, the Minister of Marine, announced that "I hope by the close of the present executive's term on November 15th, 1910, we shall see in Rio de Janeiro's harbour not less than two new battleships, two new scouts and ten destroyers." The Minister of Marine's promise was to be fulfilled, although under unhappy circumstances.

The first of Brazil's Dreadnoughts was handed over formally by Armstrongs on January 5th, 1910. It was bitterly cold on the Tyne when the new flag was hoisted "amid much

enthusiasm", a guard of honour presented arms, and a salute
of 21 guns was fired. The gun trials were a great success, the
heaviest broadsides ever fired by a battleship being witnessed
by admiring foreign naval observers, including the Argentine
naval attaché. The voyage to Brazil of the *Minas Geraes* was
mainly uneventful, although she diverted to Norfolk, Va., in
order to escort to Rio de Janeiro an American warship taking
home the embalmed body of the late Brazilian ambassador
to Washington. The journey to Brazil eight months later of
her sister ship, the *Sao Paulo,* was, however, marked by an
incident that was to have serious consequences. On October
5th, 1910, the *Sao Paulo* anchored in the Tagus alongside the
Portuguese fleet in order to take on board as a passenger
Brazil's President-elect, Marshal Hermes de Fonseca, who
was staying with King Manoel. The new battleship, possessing far greater fire power than the entire Portuguese navy,
was also five times the tonnage of the largest warship present,
and made an impression of overwhelming size and power.
That evening, while Marshal Hermes was dining at Neces-
sidades Palace the Portuguese fleet, with the exception of a
single cruiser, broke into mutiny as part of the republican
revolution and overcame or murdered their officers. A bombardment was opened on the city by the insurgent warships,
damaging the palace, the ministry buildings and a church,
and killing some one hundred people. On the following day
the king fled (Queen Amelia and Queen Maria Pia were
safely at Cintra) and was sought by the sailors, among other
places, in the *Sao Paulo*. The Brazilian officers refused them
entry, however, and the battleship's 12-inch guns deterred the
Portuguese republican mutineers from defying the Brazilian
flag. But before leaving Portugal, with Marshal Hermes
safely aboard, the crew of the *Sao Paulo* witnessed by night
the bloody overcoming of the officers of the remaining loyal
cruiser, the *Dom Carlos*. A searchlight was trained on the
quarterdeck, "holding the victims in its grip," reported the
Daily Chronicle's correspondent, who was watching from a
hotel roof. "As their dark uniforms were silhouetted against

that beam of white light the hidden machine-gun whirred afresh, and the rest of the group went down . . . Every man of that little body was lying dead . . ."

The real nature of the Portuguese revolution was beyond the understanding of the men of the *Sao Paulo,* who were mostly newly-recruited negroes, little trained and little educated. Their experiences since joining the navy had been mainly bewildering, from the long and hard journey in their transport to Britain, the acquaintance with their great ironclad and the colourful ceremonials that accompanied the occasion, to the ugly violence on the Tagus—which appeared to them as a straightforward mutiny rather than an anti-monarchist political uprising. The witnessing at first hand of the massacre of ships' officers, the apparent ease with which the sailors had taken possession of their ships, and the bombardment of the city, all made a deep impression on their minds. Suddenly there had been demonstrated to them in a most dramatic manner what could be accomplished by the combined resolution of simple blue-jackets and naval artillery that was far less powerful than the weapons now in their own possession.

Except for some minor mechanical troubles, put right by the British technicians who had remained aboard the *Sao Paulo* for the journey, the remainder of the battleship's voyage was uneventful, and the expectations of Admiral Alexandrino de Alencar were fulfilled with two weeks to spare before the completion of his term of office. On the day of Marshal Hermes de Fonseca's election the two new Dreadnoughts, the new scouts and destroyers as well as older units of the Brazilian navy were all anchored in Rio de Janeiro harbour to do honour to the new president. The fleet was by a wide margin the most formidable in South American waters. But since the arrival of the *Sao Paulo* the spirit of the men had become increasingly rebellious. In the *Minas Geraes,* where conditions were as severe as aboard her sister ship, a ringleader named João Candido sprang up and fused the general dis-affection by plotting a mutiny throughout the fleet for the night of November 22. On that evening the captain of the *Minas Geraes,* Joas Baptistu Los Neves, was dining formally aboard a visiting French cruiser. When he returned to his ship at 10 o'clock he and his fellow officers were met by rifle shots. There was a brief resistance during which the captain and two of his officers were shot dead and another officer mortally wounded. This success was signalled to the rest of the fleet, and the men of the *Sao Paulo* and the other warships took possession of their vessels without further bloodshed, despatching their officers ashore. The red flag was hoisted, an ultimatum was addressed to the government, and transmitted by wireless to a naval shore station, demanding better food and living conditions, an end to corporal punishment, and an amnesty for the mutineers. At last the raw gun crews could test the power of their weapons. Intermittent fire was opened up by the two battleships, and continued throughout the night. By seven o'clock the next morning, when no reply had been received to the ultimatum, the mutineers' four most powerful ships crossed the bar into the bay and set about a more systematic bombardment, giving special attention to the forts and naval arsenal and government buildings. The fire was not very accurate. Inevitably there were numerous civilian casualties, shops were closed and all business suspended while the new president and his ministers discussed the alarming situation, and Congress warmly debated the ultimatum. There was talk of despatching several loyal torpedo boats to destroy the new Dreadnoughts, but this was opposed as wasteful, and besides the British minister protested against this course owing to the risk to the lives of the British technicians still aboard.

There followed another restless and noisy night in the capital, and soon after dawn João Candido, acutely anxious about the delay, wirelessed another message. "We express repentance," it ran, "for the action we took for our defence, and, for the sake of order, justice and liberty, we surrender our arms, confident that an amnesty will be granted to us by the national congress, and that corporal punishment will be abolished as prescribed by law." There was, however, no visible evidence of surrender so congress met again. "The sitting," reported Reuter's correspondent, "was of an excited character and several deputies came to blows." At midday the fleet disappeared from sight, and did not return to its anchorage until word reached the mutineers by wireless that congress had voted for acceptance of their ultimatum. The President then sent a deputy, one Senhor Carvalhao, out in a launch to confer with the mutineers. He found everything quiet on board the battleships: no signs of drunkenness or robbery, he reported. But João Candido, nervous and distrustful, had fled with forty of his ringleaders.

This fleet mutiny, "engineered by misguided, rough and uncultured men who did not even know what they wanted," as the president described them, was a bad start for the new administration as well as for the nation's mighty new fleet that had been built at great expense. Abroad, it caused satisfaction to Brazil's neighbours, and dismay in Britain and America that a fleet should mutiny, and then have its demands met by the authorities. Lord Brassey, deploring the absence of training and discipline among the Brazilian seamen, remarked that "it is evident that battleships are sometimes dangerous possessions for their owners."

Never in modern times had battleships been rushed into service so soon after their commissioning. But the 12-inch guns of the *Minas Geraes* and *Sao Paulo* were soon to speak again and be heard once more in the nation's capital. Two weeks after this mutiny, on the night of December 9th, 1910, a party of marines, reported by the British ambassador as "a picked regiment in which the government has always reposed the greatest confidence," mutinied in their barracks on the Island of Cobras, and took possession of the fortress. This time the president took decisive and violent action. Martial law was declared in the city and the two battleships, now newly officered, were ordered to open fire on the rebels at dawn. Throughout the morning the city was shaken by the blast of artillery as the gun crews who had so recently set their sights on the republic's capital, now trained them on their comrades. Then the mutineers, with two hundred of their number wounded or slain, signalled for an armistice, and subsequently surrendered.

These events in no way dimmed the enthusiasm of the Brazilian government for battleships and for a further expansion of their navy. Rather, the thunderous noise of recent bombardments—however deplorable their cause—had set hearts beating faster at the Ministry of Marine. The size and firepower of the third battleship, which would ensure the republic's naval superiority over its neighbours even when their own massive programmes had been completed, was discussed with renewed fervour. Armstrong's local agents in Rio de Janeiro, the Walter brothers, were kept in close touch with the progress of these discussions. These brothers had been at school at Charterhouse with Tennyson d'Eyncourt, who found "they were very good for the firm" in their agency capacity. "The two brothers were exceedingly able men," wrote Tennyson d'Eyncourt, "and the elder, Charles Walter, was the most typical Briton I ever saw in my life. Slim, elegant, clean-cut, slow and precise in speech, he always weighed his answers even on the most trivial subjects with extreme care. This greatly enchanted the quicksilver Brazilians . . . and the deliberate accents of Charles Walter had a deep effect on them."

Six months earlier the Walters had sent back word to Tennyson d'Eyncourt at Armstrongs that at the Ministry of Marine in Rio de Janeiro a decision about this third battleship was near, and that because of the Argentine's recent decision to rush through their two counter-Dreadnoughts, it would exceed in size and gunpower all previous expectations. There were hints that a naval leviathan of a tonnage contemplated by none of the great naval powers was being seriously discussed. The *Minas Geraes* and *Sao Paulo* were already longer, heavier and carried two more 12-inch guns than

Britain's own epochal H.M.S. *Dreadnought*. Since they had been laid down three years earlier the size and power of the Dreadnought-type battleship had greatly increased, and Germany was laying down battleships of over 24,000 tons with ten 12-inch guns by 1910. But at this time in the Brazilian Ministry of Marine officers who combined patriotism with the most ardent yearning for naval gigantism were making their plans for a man-of-war that would outstrip by a wide margin the gunpower and size not only of the two Argentine men-of-war, but of every German, British, American or Japanese battleship, and would settle finally any possible dispute about the future domination of South American waters. A number of variations on this ultimate theme in battleship design had been enthusiastically drawn up by senior officers in the Ministry of Marine. They had in common an emphasis on extreme statistics in all measurements, in length and tonnage, in number and size of guns both primary and secondary. The Minister of Marine, Admiral de Alencar, came up with a design calling for twelve 14-inch guns and fourteen each of 6-inch and 4-inch on a displacement of no less than 31,600 tons. Admiral Duarte Huet de Bacellar Pinto Guedes was content with a vessel only fractionally smaller but mounting guns of 16-inch calibre, a weapon that was not to be introduced into service by the major naval powers for another decade, supported by six guns of 9.4-inch and fourteen more of 6-inch calibre. These would offer a broadside of shells weighing in all 40,000 pounds compared with some 9,000 pounds for the latest American battleships.

Armstrongs responded phlegmatically to this news. As shipbuilders it was no business of theirs to question the naval policy of one of their best customers. So long as there were no technical objections to a vessel of this size and gunpower, their task was simply to submit detailed plans and secure the contract on the best possible terms, and as rapidly as possible. Their business was profits, not politics. The fact that the proposed super-Dreadnought would upset the balance of naval power in South American waters was, in fact, likely to be to

their eventual advantage. Armament firms thrived on imbalance of power, for this was a condition that led first to cor-
rection and then to imbalance again in favour of a rival. Just
this was happening on a vast scale all over Europe, and people
who made guns were getting very rich. Tennyson d'Eyncourt
welcomed this news with special delight; it was what he had
been waiting for since that tragic rebuff in Buenos Aires. He
had always been the firmest advocate of the biggest gun and
the biggest ship; gigantism appealed to the commercial and
practical, as well as the romantic sides of his nature, for no
one can give their life to the designing of great warships without becoming affected by the grandeur of great dimensions,
and the fascination of creating unprecedented power to
destroy.

There did not seem to be at this time any doubt at Armstrongs and at the Ministry of Marine in Rio de Janeiro that
Armstrongs would receive the contract for this third battleship. Relations between the two could hardly be warmer.
Since the declaration of the Brazilian republic Armstrongs
(or Vickers, to whom they delegated some of the contracts)
had built all the Brazilian navy's larger warships, and many of
the smaller vessels as well. All had given satisfaction, including the two new Dreadnoughts, which had successfully
demonstrated their power so early in their career. Tennyson
d'Eyncourt and the Walter brothers had sealed the associa-
tion even more firmly. Then in April, 1910, Admiral de
Bacellar arrived in London to lead a permanent Brazilian
Naval Commission in Europe. At fifty-eight years de Bacellar
had behind him a long and distinguished career in the navy,
serving with distinction through the 1894 troubles. His up-
right, alert bearing and light frame, as well as the formation
of his features and the heavy moustache offered a close simil-
arity with Tennyson d'Eyncourt, and the two men had indeed become firm friends during the design and construction
of the *Minas Geraes*. For several months the two men worked
in harmony both in London and in the drawing offices at
Elswick with Mr. J. R. Perrett, Armstrong's chief constructor,

on the details of the ship. By the early autumn of 1910 everything appeared to be sealed and settled when a contract was
finally signed between Armstrongs and the Brazilian Ministry
of Marine for a super-Dreadnought of over 31,000 tons armed
with twelve 14-inch guns, in conformity with Alencar's
suggestion. She would be half as big again as the *Minas
Geraes,* with a broadside one hundred per cent heavier. It
was understood that she would be named at her launch the
Rio de Janeiro, but she was referred to at the Elswick yard
simply as Design 690, or informally as "the big battleship"
which in the British, and Armstrong, tradition nicely combined brevity with understatement.

In October, 1910, at Armstrong's Elswick yard the keel
plate was laid of the biggest battleship in the world. Much
of the material for the first stage of her construction was also
assembled, and in the gun-shops work was ready to begin on
the long and delicate task of forging and machining the
vessel's twelve 14-inch guns. For the present, however, no
further work could be done. A clause in the contract carried
the unusual stipulation that the size and cost of the giant ship
must be confirmed by the new administration and the new
Minister of Marine who would take office in November. Progress on the Alencar-inspired *Rio de Janeiro* was therefore
held up until the minister's office terminated. Meanwhile
the minister-elect had, during the summer months of 1910,
been touring the European shipyards discussing naval design
and construction with the leading authorities. His name was
Admiral Marques Leäo. Being conscious of the responsibilities that would soon be resting on his shoulders, Admiral Leäo
had visited France, Britain and Germany where he had
called on warship designers at Nantes, Bordeaux and St.
Nazaire, at Barrow and Tyneside, and at the big shipyards of
Blohm and Voss and Krupps in Germany. Everywhere he
had seen evidence of the hectic tempo of the European naval
race, and had been encouraged by the evidence of faith in

2

the value and power of Dreadnought battleships among the
European powers. In Britain there were twelve Dreadnought
battleships and battle cruisers on the stocks or fitting out,
France's programme was gathering momentum, in Germany
the urgency of Admiral Alfred von Tirpitz's demands to
meet the needs of the new High Seas Fleet had resulted in
sixteen more Dreadnoughts already completed or under construction. Confidence in the deterrent powers of the battleship appeared to be universal. Had not even Austria-Hungary,
the least maritime-conscious power in Europe, recently laid
down four of the most advanced design? At Krupp's Germania yard in Kiel Admiral Leäo was warmly received by the
senior members of the design team, who had failed in their
bids for the first Brazilian battleships and, like Armstrongs,
had lost expensively in the struggle for the Argentine contracts. Here they knew that the keel plate of a Brazilian
battleship of unprecedented size armed with 14-inch guns
was about to be laid down at Armstrongs on the Tyne.
They also knew that the contract was subject to confirmation
by the new administration when it took office in November.
Krupps took a shrewd line in the discussions. They had no
experience with 14-inch naval artillery, let alone with naval
guns of 15-inch or 16-inch calibre, which had also been proposed for the Rio de Janeiro. They therefore gave their opinion
that a battleship behemoth was an unnecessary extravagance.
If the Kaiser considered that battleships of 24,000 tons armed
with 12-inch guns were good enough for the Imperial Navy
to fight the mighty British, of what use were 14-inch guns and
a displacement of 31,000 tons against the Argentine, which
did not yet possess a single battleship? Plans were then discussed for a scaled-down version of the Rio de Janeiro, armed
with the Krupp 45-calibre 12-inch gun, and Admiral Leäo
promised that when he took office in November, Krupps
would have the opportunity to submit detailed plans and a
tender. Krupps expressed their pleasure and suggested that
before his departure from Germany the Admiral would bene-
fit from an audience with the Kaiser, whose theories on naval

warfare were widely respected. The Kaiser confirmed all that Leäo had learnt at the Germania yard: the Krupp 12-inch piece of artillery could pierce any known armour plate, it was a magnificent weapon. Besides, a smaller ship with 12-inch guns would form a more convenient, manageable and homogeneous squadron with Brazil's existing battleships, and would simplify the all-important matter of shell supply. Krupps, the Kaiser assured the little Brazilian admiral, would make a fine job of the Dreadnought.

All that he had learnt in Europe, and especially in Germany, weighed heavily on Admiral Leäo when he took office at the Ministry of Marine in November 1910. The responsibilities of his post were already great. He had inherited a brand new fleet which had cost the nation close on ten million pounds, and to date had done no more than mutiny and bombard the capital city rather severely; though for all that the common people were properly proud of it. The cost of the two battleships alone had borne heavily on the country's economy, and the dockyards, harbours and shore batteries—without which they were almost useless in war—were not yet complete. Like his fellow flag officers and the late minister, the admiral was no believer in reducing the forces under his command and the status they offered him. Nor in spite of his talks with Krupps and the Kaiser had he wholly lost confidence in the country's biggest-gun-biggest-battleship naval philosophy. But he felt obliged, within a few days of assuming office, to make an announcement on the burning topic of the republic's third battleship—the mighty *Rio de Janeiro*. To the consternation of Admiral Alencar and many of his confederates in the ministry, Leäo expressed his belief that the new ship should be "a powerful unit which will not be built on exaggerated lines such as have not yet stood the test of experience". He might have been quoting the Kaiser. He then proceeded to present to his fellow officers the detailed drawings, specification and estimate of cost of Krupp's version of what the *Rio de Janeiro* should be.

News of these disturbing goings-on in Rio was transmitted

to Armstrongs by the Walter brothers. But even these suave
agents had not collected all the information Tennyson d'Eyncourt would need to counter the German counter offensive.
A vital omission was the recent conversion of the new Minister
of Marine to the 12-inch gun. Up at the Elswick drawing
offices Perrett and Tennyson d'Eyncourt therefore busied
themselves once more with further drafts of yet more plans,
still confident in their belief that their clients required the
biggest guns while perhaps welcoming a modest diminution
in size and cost. In the early spring of 1911 Tennyson d'Eyncourt set sail again, determined once and for all to settle
the deal in favour of Armstrongs. For this purpose he carried
with him no less than eight sets of plans, a veritable maze
of permutations on the Dreadnought theme, all armed with
13.5-inch, 14-inch, 15-inch or 16-inch weapons, supported by
a secondary armament that would put up a blinding barrage
of lighter artillery fire.

By contrast with the distaste he felt for the Argentine,
Tennyson d'Eyncourt had a great affection for Brazil, and for
Rio de Janeiro. "I found the Brazilians charming to deal with
and most amiable and hospitable," he noted. This final visit,
however, was to be stormy in several respects. "One of the
minor revolutions was going on there at the time, which gave
me quite a lot of unexpected excitement . . . On the evening
of my first day I went out into the great Avenida and soon
found myself wedged in an enormous crowd of restive Brazilians obviously out for trouble of some sort, with the police
trying to disperse them. A posse of mounted police came
along, upon which some of the rioters began pulling up the
manhole covers in the middle of the street." A horse then fell
into one of these traps, and, commented Tennyson d'Eyncourt, "I got back to my hotel as soon as I could."

The next day, after consulting with the Walters, Tennyson
d'Eyncourt called at the Ministry of Marine and was shown
into Admiral Leão's office. From long experience, Tennyson
d'Eyncourt understood the unpredictable and even eccentric
nature of the South Americans as warship customers. In his

time he had witnessed vacillation, prevarication and double-dealing in every degree. He had seen them barter like the natives in the bazaars, welcome delegations with old world courtesy, negotiate interminably, agree to terms and dates and then cancel proceedings abruptly and without explanation. He had seen promising deals dissolve with the fall of a minister or a government. He had seen hard-boiled salesmen from New York and Essen with the glow of success in their cheeks, and their subsequent departure in despair. Flexibility had always been one of Tennyson d'Eyncourt's strongest cards, and it was to meet almost every eventuality that he had brought with him so many alternative plans.

In the discussion with Admiral Leão that followed it soon became evident that Kaiser Wilhelm's influence had been very strong, and that the ministry was dangerously close to switching the contract to Krupps. The little admiral quoted the German view that the 12-inch gun would meet their navy's needs, that a heavy gun of uniform calibre in the battleship squadron would simplify ammunition supply, that a giant battleship was an unnecessary extravagance. The battleship the Germans could build—and build quickly—would carry twelve 12-inch guns and would cost some half million pounds less than the Armstrong ship. Tennyson d'Eyncourt put aside all the eight designs he had brought with him without a backward glance. If the Brazilians wanted a 12-inch-gunned battleship they should have one. But he was convinced of the admiral's determination to have the smaller weapon, he was certain that there remained a lingering regret that the Brazilian navy was not to have, after all, the biggest battleship in the world. Vainglorious dreams of grandeur did not fade all that easily in Rio. He left the ministry building with assurances that he would come back next day with new ideas for discussion, and returned to his hotel.

This was an occasion when the speed of Tennyson d'Eyncourt's pencil and the fluency of his mind were to prove of such value. Undismayed, he set to work in his hotel room to adapt his designs to the minister's needs. The next day he returned to Admiral Leäo's office and continued his discussions, and in the evening set to work again. "The negotiations were slow and uncertain," the Englishman confessed. But as the days passed the engaging charm and relentlessness of Tennyson d'Eyncourt began to tell. Then he timed his master stroke perfectly. Kaiser Wilhelm had told the admiral that the Krupp 12-inch shell could pierce any armour plate. Tennyson d'Eyncourt was prepared to concede this. The 12-inch gun, whether made in Germany or Britain, was a magnificent weapon. Had not the Royal Navy ordered it for no fewer than sixteen of its Dreadnought battleships and battle cruisers? And the Kaiser was indeed correct in emphasizing the value in combat of rate of fire and the deadly effect of "the hail of shells" from the smaller calibre gun. The German emperor was also wise in emphasizing the convenience of using a uniform calibre shell for all the Brazilian battleships. Tennyson d'Eyncourt also pointed out that Armstrong's Elswick ordnance plant had made more 12-inch guns than any other gun-shop in Britain or Germany. Let us therefore select the 12-inch gun, agreed Tennyson d'Eyncourt, but let there not be twelve of them, as Krupps suggested, though this was a very large number. Let there be fourteen!

A main armament of fourteen guns in seven turrets! Such a battery had never before been considered since the age of the ironclad had begun fifty years earlier. And these to be supported by twenty 6-inch and a number of 3-inch, adding still further to the effect of bristling belligerence, which was so much a part of a Dreadnought's *raison d'être*, and would require a length overall of 671 feet. Thus, argued Tennyson d'Eyncourt, the *Rio de Janeiro* would boast the highest tonnage, the greatest length, the greatest number of turrets, and the greatest number of heavy guns, of any battleship commissioned or laid down by any power and yet would at once cost several hundred thousand pounds less than the first designs. A year earlier Armstrongs had given them the *Minas Geraes,* the wonder of the naval world. Now Tennyson d'Eyncourt was offering a leviathan with half again that ship's weight of broadside. The prospect was irresistible. When British understatement and caution, which had been the keynote of all the conversations so far, was crowned by such tempting statistical hyperbole, the effect was instant. There was not a dissentient voice in the minister's office. That night Tennyson d'Eyncourt cabled home to Newcastle upon Tyne, "The ship is ours."

Tennyson d'Eyncourt's triumph appeared to be complete. He had defeated the wily Kaiser and that giant German arms predator, Krupps. He had secured the richest prize for his company. In the fields of naval salesmanship and naval architecture he had in 1911 reached almost the peak of his career. The consequences of this success were incalculable. And yet by an odd stroke of fortune one result was almost at once manifested. News had reached Armstrongs almost simultaneously with Tennyson d'Eyncourt's cable from Rio that the post of Director of Naval Construction, the highest the Royal Navy had to offer, was shortly to become vacant. The faithful Perrett cabled to Tennyson d'Eyncourt suggesting that he should apply for the post. He treated the matter lightheartedly; he was not, after all, even a constructor at the Admiralty. "At first sight," he considered, "it looked like a joke, but there could be no harm in trying." On his return home he was interviewed by Winston Churchill, the young new First Lord of the Admiralty, who confirmed his appointment. This was indeed a reward for the success of his struggles in South America. The last summit had been conquered by this brilliant salesman-designer; there was none higher.

CHAPTER TWO

The Shipbuilders

The reason why in 1911 the prosperity of the city of New-castle upon Tyne depended so much on the fortunes of a single armaments company can be traced to the birth and subsequent career of William George Armstrong. By early middle age Armstrong was already a patriarchal figure who made the world's best guns. He had begun his engineering career in the purer field of hydro-electric and hydraulic power, building cranes of high repute, and becoming one of Newcastle's richest industrialists by the age of forty. The failure of the Royal Navy to sink the Russian ships in the Black Sea led to an Admiralty order for mines "for the purpose of blowing them up". The Crimean War began Armstrong's interest in guns. Armstrong could not understand why the contemporary instruments of destruction were so primitive and ineffectual. In collaboration with Joseph Whitworth of Manchester, he worked out a design for a gun with an opening breech, which avoided the need for slow and clumsy muzzle loading, and a rifled barrel, which caused the shell to rotate and leave the muzzle spinning rapidly and travelling with far greater accuracy towards its target. The Royal Navy accepted the Armstrong gun with enthusiasm. Subsequent events, including some nasty explosions, caused the service to revert temporarily to the muzzle-loader. But the ordnance works at Elswick flourished, mainly on foreign orders, and Elswick-built Armstrong guns were to be found in warships all over the world. From the 1860s the expansion of Armstrongs and the wealth of the founder multiplied at a gratifying rate. A shipyard was set up in 1868 and Armstrongs soon held an unique place as builders of cruisers. Chile bought the first, and soon they were to be found, armed with Armstrong guns, their magazines full of ammunition from Armstrong's great shell shops, in most foreign navies.

In 1900 Armstrongs was employing over 25,000 men, when times were good. When business was slack this number was much fewer, and hardship, disease and hunger were widespread in the city. But with the robust and philosophical temperament that marked the northern working people's acceptance of industrial distress as if it were an act of God —for troublemakers were still few on Tyneside—an improvement in circumstances brought with it gratitude and thankfulness. It was Armstrong himself—their beloved despot, the patriarch who had now become a living legend in Elswick—who gave them the work when he had it for them, and although he had long since retired to the enormous mansion and estate he had built far outside the smoke-laden city, he was still the object of the working people's gratitude when jobs were again offered. Nor could the name of Lord Armstrong be forgotten for long in Newcastle, for during his lifetime or as a memorial after his death, there were provided for the delight, the improvement and convenience of the population an Armstrong Park and Armstrong Museum of Engineering, Armstrong institutions, an Armstrong statue—and many Armstrong busts—an Armstrong Road and even an Armstrong bridge spanning the Tyne. No wonder he was celebrated as a local benefactor, and deeply mourned on his death.

By Tennyson d'Eyncourt's day, Sir Andrew Noble, an equally formidable, large and whiskered autocrat-industrialist, had succeeded to the chair. During Tennyson d'Eyncourt's period Armstrong's prosperity had increased in ratio with the tempo of the arms race with Germany. The departments manufacturing guns, gun carriages and shells had

2*

been kept especially busy. The Elswick shipyards, however, had not always been working to full capacity. Besides a number of cruisers, and the *Minas Geraes* for Brazil, two Dreadnoughts for the Royal Navy had been completed by 1910. But the loss of the contracts for the Argentine battle-ships to America had been a sorry blow, and uncertainty about the size and power of the *Rio de Janeiro* had caused one of Elswick's slips to remain vacant for more than two years. This meant renewed unemployment and real hunger and suffering in many Newcastle homes. Hope of a long period of steady employment had risen when the keel plate of the Alencar-inspired *Rio de Janeiro* had been laid down in 1910, and had fallen again when the weeks passed and none of the riveters, plate-makers, blacksmiths, carpenters, plumbers and other craftsmen received any call from the works. Then almost twelve months later, early in the sum-mer of 1911, the news of Tennyson d'Eyncourt's coup filtered out from the board room of Armstrongs. Soon there would be work for everyone. Armstrongs was, after all, to build another battleship that would give security of employ-ment for several years to the labourers and the craftsmen who lived with their families in the tiny back-to-back brick dwellings rising tier by tier above the gun and shell shops, the foundries and steel plants and the berths bordering the river Tyne. The good news spread to the local cafes like "Tilney's Cocoa Rooms" (tea and a bun for one penny) and pubs. At "The Forge Hammer", "The Hydraulic", and "The Gun" the word about work was soon heard, and mulled over by those who could still afford a pint of Bass or Burton beer or a tot of rum (1½d. a nip). "They're going to start on the big ship"—"I heard they'll want blacksmiths next week"—"It's a hasty one this, they're going to be work-ing night shifts." At the little corner grocer shops—"The Workingman's Store" or "Jamiesons"—where credit was spread out generously and where much money was on the slates—the good news that there would be money coming in, that there would be porridge again for the children before school, that debts would soon be paid off, spread as rapidly among the wives and shopkeepers. Everywhere in Elswick there was evidence of a renewal of warm affection for the Brazilians, who had become so popular for the work they had provided with their *Minas Geraes*.

Then in the early autumn weeks there suddenly began to appear on the steep streets of Newcastle the welcome sight of these dark-skinned Brazilians themselves. For more than a decade, since the first Japanese had arrived to supervise, and learn from, the construction of the battleship *Yashima*, and other ships for their new navy, foreign ministries of marine had sent representatives to understudy the multitudinous skilled trades required to build a modern man-of-war. Their appearance had made Newcastle an oddly cosmopolitan city, had brought a new tolerance of foreign ways, and had, above all, brought unprecedented prosperity to many a home which opened its doors to these temporary lodgers—at a weekly boarding rate as high as a skilled craftsman could earn in a fifty-three hour week. The Brazilians, half negro, half Latin in appearance, mainly grave and earnest and courteous, but wilder in their cups on Saturday nights than any Geordie, had arrived soon after the laying of the keel plate of the *Minas Geraes,* and were about the city, adding colour to its northern greyness, for more than two years. Then they had left, with their Dreadnought. And now they were back, in greater numbers than before, with their odd colouring, their square-cut suits and large round white caps, their extravagant gestures and their helpless incoherence. They made a fine distraction and entertainment for the children, who at first followed them curiously along the streets, calling them "Nigger" with more mischief than contempt, apeing their gestures, watching through the shop windows as they underwent the strenuous pantomime of buying shoe polish or soap. But where these Brazilian technicians lodged out privately, they were affectionate and playful with the children, and much loved by them.

By October 1911, down at the Elswick employment offices

they were signing on craftsmen as fast as they could be interviewed and checked for a clean record. The big battleship was promised for the end of 1913, it was said, a shorter construction time even than the *Minas Geraes*. There would be night shifts, and overtime. The money would be running again in the cramped little houses, the men would be out of the way at last, the tradespeople would flourish. Very few of the men understood the reason for the rush : most jobs were rush jobs. They knew nothing—nor would have cared if they had—of the two Argentine battleships already laid down in their American slips. But they knew all about the new Chilean battleship, which was soon to be laid down alongside the Brazilian monster. She was going to end any remaining unemployment in Elswick when she got going. And she was a rush job too. That's what they were saying.

In November the staging started to go up, a complex maze of pine scaffolding and planking, climbing higher and higher on both sides above the keel strake and the tank frame from which the ribs of the Brazilian monster ship would soon be rising. Already even the untrained eye could judge from across the river that this was going to be a big one. And any man in the yard who cared to pace her out could see she was going to be the largest battleship they had ever built on the Tyne. Those who had done this had learned too that she was to be the biggest ever built anywhere. During those early months of construction as the word of her size spread around Elswick, a special affection for her began to become evident. "We loved them all," said one plumber, "but the old *Rio,* she was something special." Formally, she was known as 690A, in the offices as "the big battleship". Colloquially she was sometimes referred to as "the *Rio*". More often, with a touch of pride as well as affection, as "the giant". "Working on the giant" was a phrase often heard at the street corners and in the pubs of Elswick for the next two years and more. The affection and pride aroused by the battleship was to endure for more than half a century. There

are still men alive today, many living in the same houses as
they occupied then, who worked on the ship and remember
her in vivid detail and with a warm nostalgia. For their
wives, too, the big battleship continues to hold a special place
in their memories. Even among the younger and sometimes
less contented workers there was a pride of achievement in
every vessel that ran down the slip to its launching at Elswick. But the deep and enduring affection for the big battleship especially stands out in the memories of all who worked
on her, just as her towering curved ribbings dominated the
riverside skyline in the spring of 1912, dwarfing on one side
the launched warships fitting out at the quayside, and behind
her the jumble of workshops where her gun mountings and
boilers, her engines and multitudinous internal fittings were
being prepared.

By the closing months of 1912 the world-wide battleship
race was nearing its final lap, and there was constant speculation on its outcome as well as ever-increasing pressure by
navalists in Germany and Britain for ever more ships, even
greater tonnage, even greater guns. The British "We want
eight/and we won't wait" programme of· 1909 ("the
Admiralty had demanded six ships; the economists offered
four; and finally compromised on eight" was Churchill's
ironic comment) had all joined the fleet. The Agadir Crisis
might be past, yet Britain and Germany—and to a lesser extent America and Japan—were deep buried in a competitive
arithmetical Dreadnought jungle from which there seemed
to be no escape. The British banker Sir Ernest Cassel, returning from a semi-official peace-seeking mission to the Kaiser,
reported on his return : "The new Navy Law will be passed
by the Reichstag and the naval increases are serious. Under
the former programme we should have built 4, 3, 4, 3, 4, 3
(referring to the number of Dreadnoughts to be laid down
over the next years) against their six years' output of
2, 2, 2, 2, 2, 2. But if they are to build 3, 2, 3, 2, 3, 2 we cannot

build less than 5, 4, 5, 4, 5, 4 to retain a 60% superiority in Dreadnought ships over Germany . . ." Formulae of fearful complexity, involving broadside weight, speed, armour plate thickness, cruising range, cost and many other factors of competitive comparison were thrust before the public by pacifists and "small navy" cliques to make their point as well as by the navy leagues and the more jingoistic elements of the popular newspapers to press their claims. Year by year more money was squandered on these compelling and noble symbols of power, each adding a degree or two to the Dreadnought fever that continued to sweep across the world like a plague. In 1912 there were no less than sixty-three under construction, for such unlikely and un-maritime powers as Spain and Turkey and Chile, as well as the four greatest—Britain, Germany, Japan and the U.S.A.—who alone were responsible for twenty-one of them. The British-German duel continued to dominate the field, and its implications and outcome were terrible to contemplate. But if the South American game was in the minor league and in that British sportsman's amiable phrase was "only a friendly match" it had a special edge to it and a special fascination to onlookers, for here the delay or completion of a single ship could settle the score. Construction time was a vital factor. The Dreadnought-type battleship was the most elaborate and complex weapon of war ever conceived, the co-ordination of supply of material and parts and the direction of man-power alone requiring elaborate planning. Three years was the average time. American and British shipbuilders were the fastest and could lay down, launch and complete a ship in little over two years; the Japanese, who were still learning, were the slowest.

In the crucial year of 1912 the South American score, among the three serious contenders, could be summed up thus :

Chile: one super-Dreadnought building at Armstrongs, to be completed in 1914, a second to be laid down in the slip of the *Rio de Janeiro* the moment she was launched, for completion in 1915.

Argentine: two super-Dreadnoughts building in America, due to be completed in 1913.

Brazil: two Dreadnoughts already commissioned, the super-Dreadnought *Rio de Janeiro* to be completed in the autumn of 1913.

Thanks to the foresight of the Brazilian Ministry of Marine, that nation was for the present undisputed sovereign of the South American seas, and her lead over Chile was assured for the foreseeable future, although an alliance between Chile and the Argentine could upset all these calculations. The immediate threat came from the south, from the Argentine. Her two battleships were first planned to be of 19,000 tons; then their size had been increased to 25,000 tons (it was to be increased again, though the Brazilians did not yet know this), so that, if they were commissioned before the *Rio de Janeiro* their superior gunpower to the older Brazilian Dreadnoughts' (a broadside of twelve 12-inch against ten) and more up-to-date equipment would regain for the Argentine republic statistical naval superiority.

For the Brazilians, then, everything rested on the speed with which Armstrongs could complete the big battleship, with its enormous advantage in gun power. While present relations with the Argentine were perfectly satisfactory, and no threatened dispute darkened the horizon, the Brazilian government, as if dreaming wistfully of some mythical Trafalgar played out to the music of heavy artillery fire—fourteen deafening guns in a broadside, *no one* could match that!—instructed Admiral Leäo to hasten the completion of their leviathan. From his London headquarters, Admiral Bacellar entrained for Newcastle to press for speed.

To the consternation of the Brazilian admiral, he found that Armstrongs were in difficulties. For the first time there was a shortage of skilled labour in certain trades, brought about by the huge increase in the British naval programme.

Riveters especially were in short supply, and some rival ship-yards on the River Clyde in Scotland were actually offering inflated wages and drawing away their men. There was a coal strike, too, and this was delaying the delivery of the armour plate—five thousand tons of it—from Armstrong's steel works near Manchester. The delivery date in 1913 was already jeopardized, although Sir Andrew Noble assured the Brazilian admiral that every effort would be made to make up the lost time when the material and labour situations improved.

If there was anxiety in Rio de Janeiro about the progress of their big battleship, there was deeper concern in Argen-tine naval circles about the progress of their own two super-Dreadnoughts and about the heavy balance of superiority Brazil would maintain with the delivery of its third ship. In May 1911, soon after the signing of the contract between Tennyson d'Eyncourt and Admiral Leäo, there had been new agitation in Buenos Aires for ordering a third ship—a super-leviathan a giant giant super-Dreadnought that would dwarf and out-gun even Brazil's proposed giant. Her guns would certainly be of 16-inch calibre, her tonnage at least 32,000. "The temper of the country favours the very largest," reported a correspondent for *The Times,* "and there is a strong aspiration to add still another battleship."

The months passed, work was started on the *Rio de Janeiro* by Armstrongs, and little more was heard publicly for the present about these third and fourth ships. Relations between the two republics remained as amiable as ever. In July 1912 the Buenos Aires newspaper *Jornal de Commercio* reported a speech by General Julio Roca, the Argentine Minister in Rio, in which he spoke warmly of the nations being "traditionally bound together, their armies and stan-dards having mingled in historic wars, their efforts having been united in struggles against the caudilism of La Plate." Brazil and the Argentine must remain united now and in the future, said the general, amid cheers—a sentiment that was typical of the happy tone of all exchanges between the countries. But by October of the same year when reports were received that construction of the *Rio de Janeiro* had been accelerated so that the original date of launching would be met after all, there was another bout of muscle-flexing down in Buenos Aires. It was "absolutely necessary" that the Argentine should order a third battleship, claimed Dr. Adolfo Davila, the proprietor of *La Prensa*. And the local correspondent of *The Times* reported that "the Senate would see with pleasure the government using its authority to contract for the construction of a third Dreadnought." Shortly after this the Senate passed a minute approving of this recommendation, by a majority of 15 to 7. But this time there were others who strongly opposed further naval extravagance. One of the most energetic "small navy" men was Senator Lainez, the proprietor of the principal evening paper in Buenos Aires, *El Diario*. In a leading article he spoke out "against the folly of falling into the fashion of living in armed peace". What the country needed above battleships against a mythical foe were maternity homes and hospitals, roads, and railways and bridges. There were, he pointed out, only 116,000 children attending school in the city out of a total of 300,000.

Here spoke a voice of sanity at last. Even for the great powers, battleships were appallingly expensive symbols of grandeur. Since the opening of the naval race with Germany in 1900, the British naval estimates had risen from £27m to nearly £50m. South American rivalry was costing the leading competitors—Chile, Brazil and the Argentine—almost twenty-five per cent of their national income. And the expenditure did not halt when the last cheque was paid to the builder: this was only the beginning. Besides the construction and maintenance of docks and harbours and fixed defences, the upkeep of a Dreadnought worked out at around a quarter of a million pounds a year. These three South American republics had already committed themselves to some twelve million pounds worth of battleships and many millions more on lighter craft. So far the bills had been paid on time, but the international banks were watching the situation carefully. Confidence in the credit of Turkey, for instance, in the throes of the First Balkan War, had fallen so low that Vickers had ceased work on the battleship they were building for her.

Now in the autumn of 1912 there occurred the first quiet flutters of anxiety about Brazil's economic situation and her ability to pay for her big battleship. Taxation could be raised no higher. Already recent increases were bringing about real suffering among the peasantry and city workers, and disorders such as Tennyson d'Eyncourt had witnessed often occurred in Rio and Sao Paulo. There was no material evidence of a slump yet, and in fact the trade figures revealed an economy that was still booming after dragging itself out of the coffee-surplus crisis of 1906. The danger signals this time were evident not to the international coffee brokers, but to those in the City and Wall Street who understood the Rubber market. Some years earlier a British-inspired enterprise had succeeded in smuggling out of Brazil a number of wild rubber plants from one of the great estates. These were brought back to Britain quite illegally, and cultivated under artificial conditions at Kew Gardens. Here they were bred satisfactorily until there were sufficient to transport with great care out to Malaya, where they soon flourished in specially prepared plantations. These plantations multiplied and were enlarged. The rubber could be tapped more efficiently and cheaply from plantations than from the jungles of Brazil. Soon rubber from Malaya and other parts of southeast Asia began to undercut Brazilian rubber. In 1912 a few far-sighted prophets could foresee disaster ahead for Brazil. In that year the value of Brazil's rubber exports could have paid for three *Rio de Janeiro*'s; by 1913, it was feared, the foreign income for rubber would scarcely pay for one.

In October, 1912, while the Argentine government was planning its new Dreadnought counter-stroke, progress on

the *Rio de Janeiro* was continuing apace, and she was plated
to her upper deck. Now, for the first time, her immense
length and bulk could be judged. Through the maze of
stagings and ladders and tower cranes and gantries her
cocooned hull could be seen, vast and formidable, dark grey
agains the lighter steel grey of the Tyne and the grey Northumberland sky. Except for the pause in the early summer,
there had rarely been fewer than eight hundred men at work
on her, operating shifts through the day, and at night by gas
or electric light in the workshops. In the great loft the shipwrights and template makers had prepared patterns for the
frame spacings from the complex profile drawings and
scrieve boards. Amid a heat and noise that bewildered and
deafened any stranger, the ribbings and the shell plates were
bent by hydraulic rams under the heat of fierce furnaces and
forged and stamped in the platers' shop and frame shop, the
anglesmiths' and blacksmiths' shops. From outside the
platers' shop overhead gantry cranes raised in turn the plates
that had earlier been cast in the foundries and stacked like
massive slices of grey toast, dragged them inside to be bent
and joggled, scarfed and punched, sheared, drilled and
countersunk. In the saw mill and joiners' shop, in the rig-
gers' loft and pattern shop the noise and heat and filth were
less, the products less overwhelming in size: hawse pipes
and shaft brackets, water-tight doors and valves, decking and
teak armour plate backing, companion ways and rails and
other less brutish and less impersonal parts. One by one the
big ship's ribbings were marvellously raised and carried out
to have their bracket plates fitted and lifted farther down to
the primitive skeleton in the building berth, to which they
were fitted and riveted. The shell plating followed, decently
shrouding and sealing over the rib cage and its connecting
frame stage by stage in overlapping strakes.

Seen from the Gateshead side of the river, where mist and
smoke often obscured the presence of the workmen, the *Rio
de Janeiro* appeared to be suffering the long and complex
process of ribbing, plating and decking by some sort of

remote control. Day by day the flesh seemed to be drawn more completely over the skeleton like some magic reversal of the processes of decay. Then above the upper deck there began to sprout further framing, vestigial bridgework and superstructures, forward and admidships, all seemingly planted unaided by derricks and winches and the ponderous great tower cranes. The sounds of activity, of riveting and hammering, of the crash of steel against steel, of the steady thunder of straining engines, continued ceaselessly. Only on a clear day could the eye discern the figures, like locusts swarming over the skeleton remains of a wild animal's prey. But they were there, in their hundreds, from dawn to dusk, and at night as well, working by primitive electric or acetylene lights.

As always, it was the riveters—the infantry of the working force—who were most in evidence and the creators of the most noise. They were everywhere, hard up against the plating interminably riveting steel to steel. Below them in little conspiratorial groups were the rivet-heaters, stirring their fires with bellows, turning to a glowing scarlet their lengths of steel, and then tossing them with invariable accuracy and speed up to the rivet-catchers above, who caught them in tins for rapid insertion and hammering. It was a marvellous non-stop performance. To anyone who paused in the yard and watched this process—or a dozen more of like skill —the deftness and rhythm had a spell-binding fascination.

Even before she was framed out more men were at work on the inner plating, on the bulkheads, the coal bunkers and engine and boiler seatings, the magazines that were to store more cordite and shells than any vessel before. Plumbers were at work in two shifts threading their intricate vascular system, with multiple side branches, through bulkheads and decks, from stem to stern, from bridge to boiler rooms. The electricians moved in—some two hundred of them in all at one time—to mark off the main ring all round the ship, and later to fit the junction boxes and bulkhead glands. Much of the material was laid out in orderly disarray beside the railway lines and beneath the overhead cranes on each side of the *Rio*'s berth, ready to be drawn on at every stage. Nearby in the Elswick shops the other fittings were being made ready —stanchions, davits and derrick gear from the blacksmiths' shop, the derrick posts and the great steel tripod masts—an identifiable characteristic of a British-built Dreadnought— from the mast yard, the shroud and stay wires from the rigging loft, the doors and the numerous other wooden fittings from the joiners' shop.

By November 1912 the big battleship, now within two months of her launching, had acquired much of the form and silhouette of the man-of-war she was due to become a year hence. From her fine curved stem, along the length of her unusually long forecastle, to her quarterdeck and her graceful stern—still to be embellished with her admiral's walk— she was at once identifiable as a battleship. Her twenty-two boilers were already in place, her Parsons' turbines were ready for installation. Her twin funnels and casings were almost ready for hoisting aboard, and much of her bridge structure was in position, ready to receive her armoured conning tower, searchlights and the delicate signalling and communications equipment that made this the heart of the vessel.

But seven great cavities like toothless gums scored into the centre line of the battleship, two forward, two amidships and three aft, revealed that the *Rio de Janeiro* had still to grow her teeth. This steel structure more than 670 feet long and 89 feet wide, the powerful turbine engines deep down beneath the funnel trunks, the intricate cells of watertight bulkheads and compartments, the pipes and tubes and wires than had been so skilfully threaded through the length and breadth and depth of the ship, together made up nothing more than a steel platform for the guns that were her sole *raison d'être*. The artillery: the fourteen 45-calibre 12-inch guns that would fire every half minute a total weight of

11,900 pounds of high explosive, the twenty 6-inch and ten 3-inch guns designed to support them and to fight off swift light craft—these had still to be completed and hoisted aboard after launching.

The Armstrong ordnance shops were the most famous in the land, and here the tradition of quality gun-making went back to the first days of modern artillery. There were more than forty large workshops in the ordnance works at Elswick. Here the long and expensive process of casting and forging, turning and hardening, boring and wiring, had begun as soon as the armament of the big battleship had been agreed. One by one the forty-five feet long barrels had been created from the solid-cast ingots, linered and passed through the delicate process of rifling, and of wiring with more than a hundred miles of steel ribbon to resist the bursting strain that had caused so many catastrophes with the early breech-loading Armstrong guns. Towards the end of 1912 the first guns had been erected complete with their mountings. In the largest shop of the ordnance works 28 foot deep pits had been sunk into the ground so that up to four twin turrets, each weighing some 350 tons, complete with ammunition hoists and hydraulic machinery, could be erected and tested for operation as if they were aboard their ship. By the end of the year much ordnance work remained to be accomplished. But already the first guns had been disassembled from their turrets, hoisted aboard special twelve-wheel railway trucks, and taken out to Armstrong's proof range at Ridsdale high up on the moors. Here in this lonely spot, with its vast magazines sunk into the hillside, its bomb-proof cells, its targets and armour test plate, the big battleship's guns were proved for accuracy, muzzle velocity and bore pressures along the length of the barrel. Firing in turn, their shock waves flattened the bracken and heather, their thunder echoed far across the Cheviots to Morpeth to the east and Newcastleton to the west.

These were the proving trials, the fertility rite of every piece of ordnance, to reassure the metallurgists, the chemists, and the architects, and the Brazilian officers who were buying them at such huge cost, that these 12-inch pieces could reliably hurl an 850-pound shell 24,000 yards, and within a margin of error of some one hundred feet. One by one these long sinister steel weapons were passed as fit for their role, hoisted back onto their long wagons, and drawn back over the moors down to Newcastle ready for checking and then fitting again into their mountings and turrets.

January is normally a wickedly cold month in Newcastle upon Tyne. Often the wind comes bitterly off the North Sea and is funnelled up the mouth of the Tyne and no one remains out of doors for pleasure. The month of January in 1913 was an especially cold one. There were still three hours of winter darkness when the men on the day shift got up from their beds. They dressed in their woollen linings and trousers, their two-piece overalls, and inevitable mufflers and caps, to the sound of the wind and the clatter of hobnail boots on the cobbles beneath their windows. Still unshaven, they let themselves out of their little brick terrace houses in Whitworth Street and Myrtle Place, Armstrong Road and Clara Street, and hurried downhill, guided by the widely-spaced gas lamps. In Westmorland Road, and close to the Elswick gates in Scotswood Road, brighter lights shining through patterns of stained glass drew the men towards the first comfort of their day. The pubs were legally permitted to open at six o'clock, five minutes before the works' gates were finally locked shut. The timing might have been designed to encourage speed and precision in the working men. It certainly encouraged the landlords to offer the speediest service in the city. As six o'clock chimed out on the city's clocks, the doors were thrown open and the men poured in. The offerings were simple; there was not much time for choice. Neatly ranged along the length of the bar were thick cups of strong tea and coffee and nips of rum or whisky. At the risk of scalded lips and throats there was just time for both, the debt being chalked up. Then amid the sound of voices calling out in greeting and brief ribaldry, the men burst out into the darkness and ran towards the yard—to the bright lights and the thunder of machinery.

There was less distress in Newcastle that winter than for many years. Almost every able-bodied man had a job. Besides the big battleship in her own berth, there was the Chilean Dreadnought growing apace beside her, the promise of another, besides an Admiralty contract for a super-Dreadnought of a new type, and a cruiser on the stocks. Down river at the old Walker plant, the site had been cleared and work was well advanced on a new yard to accommodate the largest ships likely ever to be built. Everywhere there was evidence of booming industry and prosperity: and if it was a cold winter, then spring would soon be here.

In the fifteen months since her keel plate had been laid the big battleship had become something of a monument, even a shrine of local affection. You could not work on any vessel for up to ten hours a day for 5½ days a week—sometimes seven days, with overtime—without becoming attached to her. When she was everywhere known as the biggest battleship in the world, and even to the layman's eye was quite evidently an exceptional leviathan, there inevitably developed a special loyalty and fondness. Her launching on January 22nd was therefore looked forward to with eagerness. Among those especially curious to see the vessel take to the water were the ambassadors, naval attachés and heads of foreign naval missions from other powers hotly engaged in naval rearmament, and especially those from the South American republics whose security was supposedly threatened by the big battleship. In accordance with the friendly sporting spirit in which the South American naval race had always been conducted, these representatives received cards of invitation to the Tyneside festivities on January 22nd. Captain Alfredo Santander, the Chilean naval attaché, accepted with pleasure. And so, of course, did Captain Luis Lan of the Argentine Naval Commission in Europe, together with his wife. Captain Lan had heard that the *Rio de Janeiro* was to be launched in an unusually advanced state of completion, and there were officers in Buenos Aires anxious for confirmation of this and for any details of the big battleship's design which they might not yet have learnt. In addition, invitations were dispatched to the appropriate officials and their wives of the London embassies and consulates of the U.S.A., Italy, France, Germany, and other powers besides the South American republics. For Brazilian prestige, this was to be a great day, a day on which the decline of the rubber market and fiscal anxieties could be forgotten.

It was also to be a momentous day for Tyneside shipbuilding, and Armstrongs properly rose to the occasion. No one knew better than they how to put on a good show for their best customers, how to flatter the vanity of minor officials as well as their chiefs, how to deal with the protocol and formalities associated with a major launching. The Brazilian contingent was of course a formidable one. Besides Admiral de Bacellar, and his wife who was the guest of honour and was to perform the ceremony, and the Brazilian Chargé d'Affaires Sr. Guerra Duval, Dr. Rodrigues Alves Filho, the Legation Secretary, Dr. Alvaro da Cunlia, the Consul in London, the senior officers and their families from the naval delegations in France, Germany and Italy were all to present themselves.

This considerable party with their servants and luggage assembled at King's Cross station on the afternoon of January 21st, 1913, where a special Pullman train awaited them. Their host on the train was Sir Andrew Noble, who saw that their comforts were attended to on the long journey north and supervised the administering of champagne after tea had been served, and later took his place at the end of the long table in the restaurant car where a seven-course dinner of appropriate splendour was served. The Royal Station Hotel, a grey granite monolithic block in the centre of Newcastle, housed in formal if chill luxury the entire entourage for the night, and on the following morning a tour round the Elswick gun-shops and shipbuilding yards was arranged for the gentlemen and for those ladies who cared to accompany them.

Many of the men who witnessed the launching of "the giant" can vividly remember the occasion today. According to custom it was a day of festivity and celebration for those who had worked on her, and for their families. They came in their Sunday-best black suits with scarves wrapped tightly round their necks, their wives in wide-brimmed hats, along with many thousands more of the citizens of Newcastle. The tickets for the seats in the specially erected grandstands flanking the slipway had been disposed of days before, and many men who were determined not to miss the occasion had climbed the stocks and scaffolding and ladders, some hanging precariously in their cold exposed positions above the ship's long forecastle deck. Mr. H. G. Amer's celebrated brass band cheered the expectant but cold crowd with rousing martial airs.

For a single group of men, on this one day a special *corps d'élite* with great responsibilities, much work remained to be done. These were the shipwrights, who had already performed the "setting-up"—the laying of molten tallow, soft soap and train oil to the touching surfaces of the slipways. By mid-day these shipwrights, working in two long lines under the direction of the shipyard manager, had driven up the wedges and transferred the whole weight of the ship from the building support blocks to the launching ways. Soon after three o'clock the signal was given by the manager for the shipwrights to split out the remaining keel block caps and to ram out the bilge blocks until the vessel was precariously held between the ground and the sliding ways only by the dog shores. This was the most precarious and important moment in the big battleship's construction, when a slight miscalculation of friction coefficients, weight and gradient could cause disaster. Too much lubricant, or under-estimation of wind strength, or a multitude of other hazardous factors, could cause the hull to slide away, not only before the ceremonial formalities but before every provision had been completed for checking her by the cables from plunging across the narrow river.

At the Royal Station Hotel luncheon had been taken, and soon afterwards the guests, well wrapped against the cold— the officers in long greatcoats with heavily goldbraided epaulettes—were helped into the limousines that awaited them in a long line in the forecourt. It was a grey afternoon, with a light chill wind, as they drove off down Neville Street and Scotswood Road towards the yard. Above the bows of the battleship a covered platform had been erected and draped with velvet curtaining, its floor carpeted, the national flags of Britain and Brazil flying above. Soon after three o'clock the ceremonial party began to assemble here, the most prominent figure being Sir Andrew Noble, a more heavily-built man now, his flowing moustache and prominent side whiskers whiter, dressed in a frock coat and top hat. He was an old hand at these occasions, and he conducted himself as host and master-of-ceremonies with self-confident aplomb. Beside him was the short dark dumpy figure of Madame Huet de Bacellar, to whom Sir Andrew presented a bouquet of pink roses, carnations and ferns while the last technical acts were conducted below.

Beside the slip the two long lines of shipwrights were waiting with sledge hammers at the ready. The crowd, and even the band, were silent now. For this was the supremely delicate moment for the shipyard manager, when he could calculate how many more minutes on land remained to the battleship only by the tone of the creaking from the stressed timbers. When he judged that the crucial moment was imminent, he raised his hands and put a whistle to his lips. Word passed up to the launching platform, to Sir Andrew Noble himself, and thence quietly to Madame de Bacellar, who stepped forward and named the ship in Portuguese—"I name you *Rio de Janeiro* . . ."—and deftly swung the bottle of champagne, decorated in ribbons of Brazil's national colours of blue, green and gold, at the battleship's stem.

Out of sight below the party, the manager put out his hands and then let them fall. There came the sound of swift blows, a lever was pulled that set into motion two hydraulic rams that knocked out the last of the dog shores, and at once the battleship began to move—"steadily and gracefully," recorded a reporter from the *Newcastle Daily Journal,* "traversing the ways at an ever increasing speed. She reached the water without a hitch, and hardly had the din subsided before she was pulled up and turned preparatory to being brought alongside. It was an impressive spectacle, worthy of the attention of the thousands who saw it from both banks of the river."

In midstream the greatest battleship ever built had been checked by massive cables after her brief period of freedom, and lay stationary in the grey waters of the Tyne, her sliding ways floating unheeded about her, the bunting that traversed her length from stern post to mastheads to prow fluttering in the breeze. Bold little tugboats appeared, nosing her gently then drawing her towards her mooring. Mr. H. G. Amer's brass band struck up with the Brazilian national anthem. Already the dim winter light was fading, and the crowds dispersing towards firesides and tea. The ceremonial platform, now poised ridiculously above only a canyon littered with irrelevant remnants, was deserted. Sir Andrew Noble, Admiral and Madame de Bacellar and the rest of the party "having remained for a few minutes in unconscious admiration of Elswick's latest triumph" had gratefully left their exposed position for the shelter of the mould loft.

In the loft the champagne was ready, and from another platform, carpeted and decorated with bunting and potted plants, the customary toasts were made. Sir Andrew thanked Madame de Bacellar for performing the launching so gracefully, referred to Armstrong's long and warm relations with the Brazilian republic (had they not had the pleasure of building ten warships for the nation in as many years?), and inevitably referred to the extreme statistics of the *Rio de Janeiro* —her length, her tonnage, her power to destroy. Then in deference to the Chilean naval attaché who was standing only a few yards away, and for whom he was also busily building a battleship, added not quite accurately, "although the *Almirante Latorre* (as she had now been renamed) will compare with her in respect to dimensions, displacement and power". Further compliments were exchanged, further toasts made in Portuguese and in English, and then Admiral Bacellar arose to speak. It was a mainly uncontroversial address, but strains of mild jingoism were introduced when he referred to the potential wealth of his country, the need to protect it "by the continued augmentation of our fleet", and to his hope that his country would be building its own super-Dreadnoughts "in the not too distant future".

Early that evening, as the arc lights were switched on in the yard for the night shift and work began on the preparation of the *Rio de Janeiro*'s vacated slip for the keel plate of her next rival, the second Chilean super-Dreadnought *Almirante Cochrane,* the Pullman train with its complement of diplomats, industrialists, politicians and naval officers drew out of Newcastle Central station for London. More champagne, and another splendid dinner, were served *en route* to the now weary party. It had been, as the press wrote of it, a most splendid day for Newcastle and for the Brazilian navy.

CHAPTER THREE

The New Owners

Until July of 1913 the regular Brazilian payments for the big battleship had been promptly delivered. The national enthusiasm for their Dreadnought was as excited as ever: in a few months time she was due to join the *Minas Geraes* and *Sao Paulo* to form a Dreadnought battle fleet more powerful than those of any nation in the world after Britain, Germany and the United States. On July 28th a banquet was held in Newcastle by Armstrongs, the guests of honour again being Admiral de Bacellar and his wife. The admiral had received orders to return home. Toasts were drunk, speeches of inordinate length were made, flavoured with regrets, with gratitude and cordial farewells. Gifts were exchanged, the admiral presenting "a fine dark bronze" to Sir Andrew Noble. It was sad to depart, said the admiral. It had been a most happy and fruitful time in Britain. What a pity that after five years he must leave with his task yet uncompleted. "But I am a fighting sailor," said Admiral de Bacellar, "and after five years in a technical capacity, it is time to return to an active fighting command."

These had been brave words. Within a few weeks the unexpected withdrawal of Admiral de Bacellar could be better comprehended. Brazil did not want her big battleship after all: she could not afford it, the money had run out. The fall in rubber exports, caused originally by British-sponsored enterprise, had proved too much for Brazil's exchequer. In February 1913 the rubber export duty had been reduced in an effort to keep in the competition with Malaya and the East Indies: it was reduced again in October. On May 5th Brazil floated a loan "of unprecedented size". It was for £11m, and there was not much interest in it. *The Times* financial correspondent commented that "the reception accorded to it seemed anything but favourable, the scrip being offered at a discount". During the summer expenditure was progressively cut back. Inevitably, reluctantly, the economy drive reached the offices of the Ministry of Marine. By an unhappy irony of fate, it was Admiral Alexandrino de Alencar, himself the most fervent monster battleship advocate and now back in office as Minister, who was forced to make the decision. De Alencar attended a meeting of the Senate Budget Committee, and afterwards announced the sad news. It had been decided, he said, that "the design of the ship did not harmonize with the organization of the fleet", and that they had decided to sell the big battleship to the highest bidder. Later it was made known that the *Minas Geraes* and *Sao Paulo* might also be for sale. So the whole Brazilian battleship fleet was to go: it was the greatest abdication of power ever recorded in naval history. At once among the South American republics, the battleship fever died. The Argentine Minister of Marine eased the pressure on the Fore River Company at Quincey, Mass. and the New York Shipbuilding Company for delivery of their two battleships. The great South American battleship race was over before two of the contestants had even received their weapons.

Meanwhile, naval authorities everywhere speculated on the outcome of an international auction for the most formidable single weapon of destruction in the world. At a time when all the major powers and most of the lesser nations too were continuing to re-arm at an unprecedented rate, the result would indeed seem to be interesting. The reserve, it was understood, was £2,750,000—the main lots (to be sold together) being assessed as to £850,000 for the hull, £420,000 for the armour plate, and £900,000 for the guns. At

Newcastle, some 800 men were at once laid off without notice, and the Directors of Armstrongs hastened to London to consult on the political implications.

The big battleship had been brought into being by the late Poet Laureate's cousin and by the patriotic enthusiasm of a group of Brazilian naval officers. She had been constructed and now almost completed by thousands of Tyneside's highly skilled tradesmen. Her future destination was to be decided by a number of notable statesmen and international bankers, and by an ambitious and plucky Turkish naval officer, Raouf Orbay.

The decline of naval rivalry in South American waters was matched by a sudden and severe increase in the Mediterranean. Armament manufacturers had no cause to fear for loss of business, and the South American republics soon found eager customers for any unwanted warships. For in the Mediterranean, naval competition was real and earnest. Here battleships were for fighting rather than for amiable games of beggar-your-neighbour, for Presidential review, and an occasional mutiny. Passions ran deep and the sound of war drums was all too audible through the jungle of power politics, aggrandizement and religious conflict. In September, 1911, there had begun a squalid little war between Italy and Turkey over Italian colonial policy in Tripoli. A year later, after a shattering defeat, the Turks were at it again, this time against Serbia, Bulgaria, Montenegro and Greece. It was called the Balkan War, and if possible was more ignoble and beastly than the business with Italy. In both wars the Ottoman Navy, with a single shining exception, took a sporadic and discreditable part.

The Imperial Ottoman Navy had been quietly rotting away in its own corruption since the Russian war of 1877-8. In 1903, the Earl of Selbourne, the British First Lord of the Admiralty, described the Turkish navy as "non-existent, absolutely and without qualification." In 1904 a British admiral, Mark Kerr, had reported on the condition of the fleet and dockyards in similar terms. "It is no longer possible to talk about the Turkish navy," he wrote, "as it is practically non-existent."* He told of dissolute admirals living ashore, of ships stripped of saleable accessories rusting in dockyards, of vital or lethal parts taken ashore and stored, against the fear of mutiny or revolution, in the Sultan's palace. Admiral Mark Kerr as sweepingly condemned Turkish personnel. "The Turk is not a sailor by instinct, neither has he any belief in Heaven's first law—order, and consequently never can become the combination of a seaman and a mechanic that goes to make the modern man-of-war's man." Later, Mark Kerr took on the task of reorganizing the Greek navy, and left others to do what they could to revive the decaying corpse of Ottoman sea power.

The date of Admiral Mark Kerr's and Tennyson d'Eyncourt's official inspections of the Turkish navy coincided with the first evidence of a mild naval renaissance on both sides of the Aegean. The old conflict between Moslem and Christian in the Balkans and the eastern Mediterranean was once again precipitating Greece and Turkey towards war. Both nations carefully took stock of their naval power and found it wanting. As alert as the most sensitive diplomat for hints of future violence, the British, German, American, French and Italian armament manufacturers soon had agents in Athens and Constantinople at work offering contracts. The past record of British companies in this part of the world was mixed. Both the Greek and Turkish navies admired British torpedo craft, and many of Turkey's larger coastal defence craft had been built in Britain in the 1860s and 1870s. But Krupps had more recently made headway, and French, Italian and even American yards were becoming increasingly competitive. Armstrongs had succeeded in getting a contract for a new Turkish warship—the *Hamidieh,* a cruiser which, with the royal yacht and state barge, Tennyson d'Eyncourt had handed over officially to the Turkish Ministry

* *Land, Sea and Air* by Admiral Mark Kerr (1927)

3

of Marine in 1904. Subsequently, Tennyson d'Eyncourt's powers of salesmanship, and evident qualities as a designer, were largely instrumental in persuading the Turkish Ministry of Marine to buy British in the new naval race that gathered tempo in the succeeding years. His chief ally in this campaign was Rear-Admiral Sir Douglas Gamble, a serving officer in the Royal Navy who was appointed in 1908 to lead a British Naval Mission to reorganize the Ottoman Navy, enlarge and modernize it with warships built in British yards, and generally to counterbalance German efforts to gain orders for arms and convert the army into a pro-German force.

Greece entered this period of tension with a much more trim and much smaller navy than Turkey's. Admiral Mark Kerr, before taking over its reorganization, found it "very peaceful, charming and clean, reminding one of the navy of the operatic stage—small, clean ships, with slack ropes and rigging, officers and men with waxed moustaches and spotless white duck trousers and small waists."* Its spirit was transformed by the energy and enthusiasm of Mark Kerr, and it was given formidable new strength through the patriotism of a shipping millionaire Giorgio Averoff who bequeathed £280,000 towards the cost of a modern man-of-war to meet the growing threat from Turkey. The Greek government found the additional £680,000 which made possible the purchase of a powerful 10,000-ton armoured cruiser, to be named after the donor.

The naval side of the Balkan War that followed was mainly cheerless and unheroic on the Greek as well as the Turkish sides. Neither navy was very keen on fighting, nor could they shoot very well, though the Greeks were not as inaccurate as the Turks. When ships sighted one another the Turks tended to retire, and the occasional exchange of shots did little damage. After a while the Turkish ships remained in harbour. But the nature of the conflict at sea was also redeemed for both sides by the performance of one of their

* Land, Sea and Air.

ships, in each case the most modern and efficient. It was the *Averoff* which by her show of aggression and accurate shooting, put the Turkish fleet to flight and by her initiative mainly dominated the Aegean. And it was the cruiser *Hamidieh,* now nine years old, which did something to redeem the Turkish maritime reputation by breaking through the Greek blockade and harassing the enemy's rear, bombarding enemy ports and interfering with troop movements like any Elizabethan freebooter. Her commander was Raouf Orbay. Raouf Bey was described by one of his contemporaries as "very young, very keen, very ambitious". He was a dark, dapper man of medium height, with hair parted in the middle and a Groucho Marx moustache. He spoke gently and always courteously, and gave an impression of sharp intelligence and a strong capacity for survival. Raouf Bey had entered the navy to further his political ambitions, which were boundless. In later years he fought his way through numerous intrigues and counter-intrigues to become Prime Minister under Mustafa Kemal and subsequently an exile. In 1912 he saw the war against the Balkan powers not only as a patriotic crusade but also as an opportunity to establish himself as a national hero. He set about this task with business-like efficiency.

Unlike other ships' companies in the Turkish navy, the *Hamidieh's* men were smart and well disciplined, and they could even shoot. The *Hamidieh's* opening engagement was a qualified success. In a night action off the Bulgarian port of Varna, Raouf took his cruiser through a line of torpedo boats, later claiming to have sunk two of them. But a third, which he damaged, succeeded in putting a torpedo into the *Hamidieh's* bows, and Raouf brought her back to the Golden Horn with her bows awash. Raouf had his ship pumped out and repaired at Constantinople with a remarkable speed for Turkish dockyard workers, and on January 14th, 1913, without orders and entirely on his own initiative, sailed into the Aegean, where he at once sank a Greek auxiliary cruiser. For many weeks he then played a skilful game of hit-and-run with the Greek navy. He steamed first to Syra, where he shelled a powder factory, a coal depot and the local power station. On the 19th he was at Port Said for coal and provisions. He sailed the *Hamidieh* through the Suez Canal, returned in February, and set about a sustained campaign of destruction and evasion, bombarding transports and troop concentrations, smashing Greek encampments, and sinking ships all over the eastern Mediterranean and the Aegean Sea. In August, three months after the Armistice had been signed, Raouf Bey returned to Turkey, to be "subjected to much fulsome press adulation and municipal feasting", as one correspondent described his welcome. The man from *The Times* went further. "The whole Greek Navy was paralysed by a single cruiser in being, and it is, perhaps, not too much to say that that single cruiser may have saved Constantinople."*

In contrast with the naval race in South America, where there was never any serious threat of war, the competition for battleships in the eastern Mediterranean did not reach its peak until the war was over. Utterly defeated on land and sea, in spite of the gallant endeavours of Raouf Bey, Turkey lost almost all her European empire. Above all, she now found herself without her vital strategic islands in the Aegean. The Treaty of London which terminated the First Balkan War was little more than a snarling agreement to disagree, while Christian and Moslem alike zealously prepared for a re-opening of hostilities. Sea power was the key to the Aegean; and power at sea was controlled by the big gun, by the battleship.

Admiral Gamble and his staff had already achieved some success in their campaign to modernize the Turkish navy before the outbreak of war with Greece. Two old German ships had been acquired, but they were no more than an inadequate and hastily-devised stopgap. Modern Dread-

* *The Inner History of the Balkan War* by Lt.-Colonel R. Rankin (1914).

noughts were needed, Gamble had told his receptive audience. Battleships had given Britain her omnipotence at sea; and the best battleships were built in British yards, of course. Besides the battleships, there would be a dozen destroyers for the newly rejuvenated Turkish navy, and about forty smaller craft. For a start, in 1911 two Dreadnoughts of the most modern type ("equal in power to the latest Royal Navy battleships" was the specification) were laid down in England, the contract being worth around £4m. Progress on the first of these had reached the protected deck before the builders stopped work on it while the outcome of the First Balkan War was decided. In May, 1913, after being financially reassured, the builders accelerated construction of the *Reshadieh*. In September, amid celebrations as joyous as those accompanying the launch of the *Rio de Janeiro* nine months earlier, the *Reshadieh* was launched by the beautiful young Naile Hanoum, daughter of the late Grand Vizier, his highness Tewfik Pasha. As this was a Moslem Dreadnought a bottle of rose water instead of champagne was smashed against her prow; then Miss Hanoum was presented with a platinum necklace set with diamonds.

Meanwhile, on the other side of the Aegean Sea, Admiral Mark Kerr, now graced with the title Commander-in-Chief of the Royal Hellenic Navy and Naval Adviser to King Constantine, was assiduously nourishing Greek naval ambitions. He had not been displeased with the performance of his protegés in the late war, for at one time or another they had put to flight every Turkish vessel that had nosed out of the Dardanelles, except the notorious *Hamidieh* and her bold commander. But the new Turkish threat, supported by his fellow Royal Navy officer—his fellow countryman, his opposite number—in Constantinople, had to be taken seriously. Mark Kerr was something of a naval radical, a man who spoke his mind and, in that telling contemporary phrase, "did not suffer fools gladly". He thought that battleships were on their way out, that lighter craft, and submarines, and even aircraft, were the weapons of the future. There was much to be said in favour of his case, but it was not an easy one to argue when every major power in the world had committed itself to the battleship as the ultimate weapon, and the theoretical balance of maritime power rested on them. The case against the battleship was a difficult one for any politician to make when so recently he had been squandering the taxpayers' money on the Dreadnought deterrent.

Mark Kerr was no politician. He thought he knew how best to meet the menace of Turkish battleship power, and went off to the King to explain his scheme. "It began by pointing out that battleships were quite useless in narrow waters such as surrounded Greece," Mark Kerr later explained, "because submarines by day and destroyers by night had made narrow waters a grave for capital ships. I made out the Greek programme in accordance with these ideas, and also laid down an air establishment which, in conjunction with a chain of wireless stations, and assisted by nets, would paralyse and destroy the submarines of a possible enemy. The King said that he had been brought up to believe in the biggest possible ship, but he wished me to argue my case. At the end of an hour he said to me, 'Admiral, you have converted me. Now go and convert my Ministers'." But Mark Kerr found the Prime Minister, Sophocles Venizelos, "an obstructionist" to his campaign, and the Minister of Marine to have "a great wish to have a battle-fleet . . . and the Greek officers generally believed in the largest ship and the largest gun".* Mark Kerr might be the C-in-C—and he did persuade the government to order four new destroyers—but within a few days of the announcement that work had recommenced in Britain on the Turkish super-Dreadnought *Reshadieh,* the Greek Minister of Marine was telling the Chamber of Deputies, amid cheers, that the navy would require two battle-cruisers—faster but less heavily armoured Dreadnoughts than battleships—"in conformity with the needs of the country".

* *Land, Sea and Air.*

This time Britain did not get the contract—and why should she when the British Commander of the Royal Hellenic Navy advocated submarines and airplanes? The Krupp salesmen were soon on the spot, and the battle-cruiser *Salamis,* to be armed with 14-inch guns (bigger than the *Reshadieh's*) was laid down at the Germania yard. But no matter how hard Krupps worked, the *Salamis* could never catch up the *Reshadieh,* due at Constantinople in the summer of 1914. What was worse, the Turks were starting work again on the *Reshadieh's* sister super-Dreadnought. There was only one answer, and that was for the Greek navy to scour the world's navies for ready-made battleships.

The summer of 1913 was not the best time to go shopping for battleships. The British and Germans, with greater fleets of Dreadnoughts than the rest of the world together, were in no mood for selling; since the Agadir Crisis of 1912 both powers were more than ever preoccupied with their ratio of deterrents. The American and Japanese navies were worried about the balance of power in the Pacific and together had nine on the stocks or fitting out. The Italians were worried about the new Austro-Hungarian battleships —four of them, of excellent quality, it was reported in the most authoritative naval circles. She had only one herself. The Spaniards were building three, and wanted them all. And it was not even worthwhile calling on the Russians. South America appeared the most likely source. These underprivileged republics could not afford them, and by no sane reasoning could they have real need for them. So representations were made through the Greek legation in Rio de Janeiro for the cash purchase of the *Minas Geraes* and *Sao Paulo.* Brazil, not yet at the end of her economic tether, turned down the offer—although this evidence of the bullish state of the Dreadnought market was noted by the government for future reference. The launch of the *Reshadieh* prompted Greece to intensify her search. Up on the Tyne the Chilean super-Dreadnought *Almirante Latorre* was soon to be launched. This time the shoppers were not immediately rebuffed. News of the Greek negotiations in Valparaiso reached Constantinople and were reported by the newspaper *Tanin*. "This is a most serious threat," ran a leader, "and to help meet it we must build more battleships." As to the expense, went on the *Tanin,* this could be met by government officials foregoing part of their arrears of salary, and Turkish businessmen should "surrender a large percentage of their profits to enable the Ministry of Marine to purchase (them)." The next day the Chilean government issued a denial that it was in the market anyway.

It was at this happy moment in October 1913 that the Brazilian government decided to inform Armstrongs that they did not want their big battleship and that it could be put up for auction. Nor did they deny reports that their other two Dreadnoughts might, after all, be for sale.

The negotiations in November and December 1913 involving the sale of the big battleship were prolonged and tortuous, and momentous in their consequences. From the beginning only two governments, the Greek and Turkish, were seriously in the bidding, although Armstrongs said that this was a world auction. It was not that the great powers did not want more battleships, and big ones at that. But none except Italy expressed interest—at least not to the tune of nearly three million pounds—in the *Rio de Janeiro*. There were curious, even obtuse reasons for this. She was the most publicized battleship in the world, and the power of her fourteen 12-inch guns was enough to overwhelm any Dreadnought afloat. But the battle fleets of the great naval powers were being built by squadrons to a careful plan of homogeneity, and the *Rio de Janeiro* could not be matched with anything afloat. So great, so freely-quoted, were the big battleship's dimensions that she was by 1913 statistically suspect, and even regarded as an experimental freak. The sheer numbers of her guns, the sheer size of her magazines, told against her as a sales proposition to anyone who was not *in extremis,* as were the Greeks and Turks. It had also been heard in some naval quarters that the Brazilians had demanded such luxurious living accommodation that her internal water-tight compartmentation was inadequate, that the size of her magazines for her great numbers of guns made her dangerously vulnerable, even that a full broadside from all those guns would break her back. Indeed in some naval circles it was hard to deny that the *Rio de Janeiro* had actually assumed certain clownish characteristics.

In their disposal of the big battleship on behalf of the Brazilian government no political pressure was brought to bear on Armstrongs. As the world's leading builders of foreign warships, Armstrongs were themselves liberally blessed with diplomacy to meet situations of this kind. They also knew everything about international banking, and through their agents in the City understood the financial standing of foreign governments with whom they did business. The exchequer of neither Greece nor Turkey was in good shape after the Balkan Wars, and it was soon evident that the *Rio de Janeiro* would go to the country that could raise the money from loans, which would in turn depend on the degree of security offered. The Greek government, recognizing that in their possession the *Rio de Janeiro* would more than offset the power of the Turkish *Reshadieh,* and that failure to acquire her would mean that Turkey would possess within some six months two overwhelmingly powerful new Dreadnoughts, made strenuous efforts to secure the confidence of a bank—any bank. During the first three weeks of December, every bank with the necessary funds in France, Italy, Germany and Britain was approached. These same European powers were appealed to on a diplomatic level in an effort to convince them of the danger of upsetting the balance of power in the Aegean. The Greek efforts met with failure at both levels.

The Turkish government was more wily and astute. A delegation from the Ottoman Treasury was dispatched to

3*

Europe to call on the leading bankers in order to persuade them of the security of Turkish credit and by the country's ability to repay the substantial loan called for by the purchase of the big battleship. At the same time the pressure was put on her adversary, the Turkish plenipotentiary, Hrant Bey Abro, travelling to Athens for talks on the disputed Aegean Islands; he made it amply clear to the Venizelos government that Turkey was determined on re-possession. Raouf Orbay, now promoted to captain, willingly lent his services to the national campaign. In September this hero boarded the *Hamidieh* once again to the cheers of a large crowd and sailed down the Dardanelles into the Aegean. He was off on a glorious flag-showing cruise round Europe to flaunt Turkish heroism and nationalism after his widely publicized buccaneering activities during the late war, which had resulted, he claimed, in such an unjust peace for the Ottoman Empire. Raouf Bey filled his role with perfect aplomb. But in England he had other business. Here his task was to use his best endeavours to hasten the completion of the battleship *Reshadieh,* and to make contact with Armstrongs to discover some facts about the *Rio de Janeiro* now that she was up for sale. It was vitally important to discover when she, too, would be ready for action, how much she was to cost, and how she was to be paid for.

Little is known of the precise nature of Raouf Bey's activities in England, and how much of the credit for the final outcome was due to his efforts and how much to the efforts of the Ottoman Treasury and foreign legation officials who were working so busily in Berlin, Brussels, Amsterdam, Paris and London. But success certainly crowned the cruise. Within a few weeks of the *Hamidieh*'s departure the French Perrier Bank announced that it had negotiated a loan of four million pounds to the Turkish government at an interest rate which, *The Times* financial page announced with evident relish, was "practically 12½%". The asking price of the big battleship was now widely known to be £2,725,000. On December 20th, 1913, the Ottoman ambassador in London opened direct negotiations with the British government and Armstrongs, and to add credence and validity to the seriousness of Turkish intentions, the Perrier Bank transferred a million pounds to London as a deposit on the purchase.

In the face of this assault, the Greek Venizelos government was helpless. They had utterly failed to justify their cause to any of the European bankers. They had appealed to France, a strong sympathizer with their cause, not only for money for themselves, but to refuse it to their enemy. They had appealed to Britain and America on the grounds that the sudden appearance of the big battleship in the Mediterranean would destroy the *status quo* so recently achieved and would lead inevitably to the reopening of hostilities. Over the Christmas period as the negotiations between Armstrongs and the Turks neared completion they added forlorn last-minute protests.

The deal was finally settled on December 28th, and on the following day the Turkish government exultantly gave the news to the world. The biggest battleship, together with its smaller partner the *Reshadieh,* would be ready for action by June 1914, or at the latest by July. She was to be known, continued the announcement, as the *Sultan Osman I,* after the first and fiercest of all the great 14th and 15th century warrior Sultans, who had subdued most of south-west Asia and north Africa; as his namesake would crush the hated Greeks five hundred years later. And she would be commanded, of course, by that hero of the late war, Captain Raouf Bey.

The Greek government recoiled from the blow with a brave face. Venizelos told the Chamber that he was determined that Greece "would remain mistress of the Aegean". Then from across the Atlantic there appeared a momentary glimmer of hope. The offer was not officially inspired; indeed, it was curiously indirect, even devious. The New York

Shipbuilding Company, as avid as ever for foreign Dreadnought orders (it had nearly finished its ship for the Argentine and no other contracts had been signed), threw out the interesting proposition that it could arrange to acquire five old battleships from the U.S. Navy, and sell three of these to Greece right away, on the understanding that the Greek Ministry of Marine placed an order for a super-Dreadnought with them. This was perhaps a time for clutching at any straw, and Venizelos said that he was interested. Officials at the Ministry of Marine investigated the offer more closely, and did not care for what they found. All the battleships involved had been designed nearly twenty years before, and were so dangerously obsolete (no wonder the U.S. Navy was glad to see the sterns of them) that against the big battleship they would be only floating coffins for their Greek crews. Two of them, the *Kearsage* and *Kentucky,* had their ancient 13-inch and 8-inch guns mounted two above two in a unique sort of two-storeyed turret, an arrangement that had surprised naval architects at the time and had not been copied abroad as the blast damage from one set of guns was liable to do serious injury to the crews manning the others. Venizelos finally said no, he didn't want them.

In spite of this set-back, which was not made public, Admiral Coundouriotis, the Greek Minister of Marine, expressed his belief that "no anxiety need be felt". The fire of maritime self-confidence was burning so brightly in Greece after the recent victories that even the threat of the fourteen big guns of the *Sultan Osman I* could not entirely extinguish it. But Venizelos, a shrewd and seasoned diplomat, was also enough of a realist to recognize that the arrival of the big battleship in the Mediterranean would lead inevitably to war, and a war which his country could hardly hope to survive. Early in January he began his first steps to correct the situation. To Britain he addressed a note of protest for allowing the sale to go through at all: it was an act of overt provocation. What did Britain propose to do by way of correcting the imbalance of power in the Aegean? As Greece had chosen to place her orders for warships with Germany, came the reply, there was little that the British government could do to correct the situation, which had been brought about by the failure of a South American republic to meet the terms of its contract with a private British company over which His Majesty's government had no control.

How soon could the *Salamis* be made ready? Venizelos demanded of Krupps. Not before the summer of 1915. The Greek Ministry of Marine had chosen American guns for their German-built battle cruiser, and they were not yet ready, nor would be for another year. However, Germany took immediate steps to hasten the delivery of six powerful destroyers, and on January 16th, 1914, these were reported to have arrived at Kiel *en route* for Athens. Venizelos reserved his strongest protest for France, her friend for so many years. How had it come to pass that the government had allowed the Perrier Bank to put up the money? The French government retorted that it had no control over the activities of the nation's bankers: this was a domestic business. It was made known to Venizelos, however, that if Greece required one or two new battleships, there were shipyards in France equipped to build them rapidly, and that any difficulties over financing them would be overcome. Greece accepted the offer eagerly, plans were drawn up for a 23,000-ton battleship armed with ten 13.5-inch guns, similar to France's own latest, and some weeks later M. Romanos, the Greek Minister in Paris, travelled to Nantes to fix the first rivet of the Royal Hellenic Government's new super-Dreadnought. The order for a second similar vessel was also confirmed.

A battle-cruiser from Germany, a pair of super-Dreadnought battleships from France: this was splendid news, a tribute to those who had negotiated these purchases, which would provide the means for the reassertion of Greek naval power by the summer of 1917. But the prospects for the summer of 1914 remained as alarming as ever. Against the biggest battleship in the world, and a second of 23,000 tons, the Greek navy would still be able to muster only one modern armoured ship of some 10,000 tons, the battle-tried armoured cruiser *Averoff* with her 9.2-inch and 7.5-inch guns. In spite of what Admiral Mark Kerr—still head of the British Naval Mission in Greece, but now quite discredited— might say about the superior fighting value of small swift ships, submarines and aircraft, big guns could be met only with bigger guns. Battleships were still needed urgently, within weeks.

Some hope for Greece came unexpectedly and from an unlikely quarter. Within eight weeks of the date at which the *Sultan Osman I* was expected to arrive at Constantinople under the command of Raouf Bey, President Woodrow Wilson of the United States, that great man of peace and upholder of the *status quo,* let it be known to the Greek Legation in Washington that the United States Navy might be prepared to sell off a couple of newer battleships, the *Idaho* and *Mississippi,* if the price was right, and if he could get the sanction of Congress. Venizelos responded eagerly. Yes, of course he wanted the American battleships. Under the circumstances the price was not important to the Greek government. Somehow the money would be found. Venizelos instructed his Minister in Washington to accept the offer, and discover when the ships could be made available. According to the latest information from London the *Sultan Osman I* would be leaving on her acceptance trials within five weeks. Were the battleships ready? Were they in good order and battle-worthy? Was ammunition for the guns part of the deal? These were the questions that passed through the Greek Legation in Washington. But above all, when could they have them? The control of the eastern Mediterranean, of the Aegean Islands, the outcome of the next round in the timeless struggle between Christian Greek and Moslem Turk depended on whether these battleships could be got to Athens before the Turkish giant arrived in the Bosporous.

Their delivery depended also on the proper democratic

processes of a United States Congress that was torn between reluctance to become a party to the dingy claims of the Balkan power tussle and alacrity to conclude a good deal when one was offered. The Administration had also to contend with the powerful "small navy" group in Congress, which saw in the Navy Department's proposal a sly means of sidetracking regular navy appropriations by a piece of sharp practice at the expense of a little Christian state with its back to the wall.

At first the President's plan looked as if it would go through without difficulty. On May 28th, Navy Secretary Josephus Daniels appeared before the Senate Committee on Naval Affairs to advise acceptance of the amendment providing for the sale of the two battleships. The amendment, offered by Senator Lodge of Massachusetts, did not name the country which wanted to buy the ships, nor state the minimum acceptable price. But everyone knew about the President's approach to Greece, and that that country was getting no bargain basement cut-price deal, that in fact Greece was not going to get them for less than the original construction cost of the vessels. The amendment was passed without controversy, several members commenting that they were doing nicely out of the transaction.

This easy passage of the first stage of authorization aroused widespread interest, and also some wry comments on the progress of technical development of modern fighting ships, and their rapid obsolescence. After all, only six years had passed since the two men-of-war had been hailed as the navy's latest instruments of destruction and as magnificent vessels carrying in all twenty guns of 12-inch, 8-inch and 7-inch calibre. "Modern warships, in spite of their enormous cost and the obduracy of the steel out of which they are made, are but little longer up to date than a spring hat of lace and flowers," observed the *New York Times*. "Neither of them has ever fired a little or big gun at anything more responsive than a floating target and each is as efficient as it was when it exemplified the highest state of naval construction. Yet already the experts sniff at both as deplorably behind the times and out of fashion, and the opportunity to get what they are worth to little Greece for possible use against her ancient enemies, the Turks, has been eagerly welcomed." Perhaps, suggested the leader writer, one could safely hail the newest Dreadnought as "Soapbubbles ahoy!"

President Wilson's peace move, in spite of its auspicious start, now suffered two setbacks. On June 16th the House of Representatives debated the amendment to the Naval Appropriation Bill. The "small navy" men were much in evidence; many of those who might have supported it were away from Washington. "The fight over the proposal ran into a night session which lasted until 10 o'clock. While the Sergeant-at-Arms and his deputies searched the city for members from 6 o'clock until ten, the business of the House remained practically at a standstill, with the parliamentary situation such that an adjournment could not be brought about. Several members started to sing. 'My Old Kentucky Home' appeared to be a favorite. Somebody started 'America' and the spectators in the galleries stood up and joined in the refrain."*

The Greek government, unable to comprehend the tortuous procedures of a liberal democracy, fretted at the delay. A month before, the course of events appeared to be plain sailing. The head of the American state wanted to help by offering the Hellenic navy two battleships. Who were these Republicans, these anti-navy Democrats, trying to prohibit this sale that was so financially advantageous to their country? The Greek Legation in Washington was asked urgently to inquire of President Wilson the reason for the delay.

The Turkish government had been dismayed at the American President's proposition, had warmly protested, and had been relieved at the success of the "small navy" minority in the Senate. Rustem Bey, the new Turkish ambassador, had just arrived in Washington, and on the afternoon of

* *New York Times,* June 17, 1914.

June 22nd he hastened to the White House to present his credentials. He naturally took the opportunity of mentioning the proposed sale to President Wilson. "To his surprise," reported the *New York Times* correspondent, "he was told by the President that he had assurances from the Greek Legation that the battleships were wanted for peaceful purposes. Earlier in the day the President had told his callers that unless he had received assurances that the warships were to be used for the preservation of peace he would not have approved their sale." The new ambassador, while expressing surprise at this response, reserved his comments for an official statement issued in the evening. "The contention that the sale of the two battleships," it ran, "will restore the naval balance between Turkey and Greece and would prevent the explosion of hostilities is faulty. If the two American battleships came into the possession of Greece before Turkey gets the two battleships now under construction for her, they will add to the considerable superiority she already enjoys over Turkey. If she gets them after Turkey gets hers, which are super-Dreadnoughts, she will fall into a state of distinct inferiority." Thus, claimed the ambassador, "the American action would miss its very honourable object, and in reality would amount to taking sides with Greece against Turkey in the naval rivalry between the powers."

The *New York Times* found President Wilson's disagreement with the Turkish ambassador "decidedly amusing". In a leader on June 24th the newspaper suggested that "a simple way, whether or not a good one, for Turkey to keep the Greeks from getting our ships would be to make a higher bid for them than the Greeks made. The President isn't part-Scotch for nothing, and that would appeal to him, perhaps more than Pickwickian talk about peace."

There was no doubt that the American Navy could have got an even more inflated price from the Ottoman government. In Constantinople Djemal Pasha, the Turkish Minister of Marine, made this quite clear to Henry Morgenthau, the American ambassador in Constantinople. Morgenthau reported, after calling at the Ministry of Marine, that he had "hardly ever seen a man who appeared more utterly worried". The subject of the proposed sale came up at once between the two men. "As he began talking excitedly to my interpreter in French, his whiskers trembling with his emotions and his hands wildly gesticulating, he seemed to be almost beside himself," Morgenthau wrote. "He begged, he implored that I should intervene. If the transaction were purely a commercial one, Turkey would like a chance to bid. 'We will pay more than Greece',"* asserted the anxious Minister of Marine.

Ambassador Morgenthau found that the Germans were almost as anxious as the Turks about the impending sale, which might well threaten a vital pivot in the German defence scheme. On the afternoon of June 13th the German ambassador, Baron von Wangenheim, "a big, overbearing cavalry officer of the Prussian type, with a graceful wife,"† and Morgenthau went riding together in the hills north of Constantinople. Von Wangenheim took the opportunity of raising the vexed question of the battleships-for-Greece deal. "Just look at the dangerous precedent you are establishing," he said. "It is not unlikely that the United States may some time find itself in a position like Turkey's today. Suppose you were on the brink of war with Japan; the English could sell a fleet of Dreadnoughts to Japan. How would the United States like that?" Von Wangenheim suddenly became quiet and extremely earnest. "There we sat on our horses," wrote Morgenthau of that afternoon, "the silent ancient forest of Belgrade lay around us, while in the distance the Black Sea glistened in the afternoon sun." The German ambassador began to speak again. "I don't think that the United States realizes what a serious matter this is. The sale of these ships might be the cause that would bring on a European war."*

* Secrets of the Bosporus by Henry Morgenthau (1918).
† Turkey: Yesterday, Today and Tomorrow by Sir Telford Waugh (1930).

Before they rode on von Wangenheim begged Morgenthau to intervene and cable the President personally.

Ambassador Morgenthau reported the situation in Constantinople to Washington, and made clear that the Turks were willing to raise their price above the Greek government's. But the matter was not "purely a commercial one". President Wilson knew as well as his ambassador in Constantinople that as soon as Djemal Pasha got his big battleship war was certain to break out again in the Balkans, unless Greece got her battleships, too.

The House debated the vexed question again on June 23rd. Presidential pressure had been brought to bear, and members had been urged to pass through the bill as rapidly as possible. Before this could be accomplished some disquieting aspects of the deal had been revealed to the Greek Legation. The Greek authorities already knew that they were paying around three times the real market value of the two pre-Dreadnought battleships; this had been made perfectly clear by advocates of the bill, who had frequently and freely used it as an argument to support their President's cause. There was worse to come. "They are undersized and slow of speed," remarked Representative Mann of Illinois. "They impair and destroy the efficiency of the whole fleet. Already we have had experience in trying to keep these two ships up with the others, and the effort broke their mainshafts." "Greece would not have been willing to pay the price unless her needs were urgent," remarked a navy official, according to the *New York Times* reporter. "In the ordinary course, the ships would be consigned to the scrap heap, or be used as targets."

At least this sort of talk offered some comfort to the Turks, who made one last formal protest. There were no vocal supporters of the Turkish cause. But voices were raised against the sale for other reasons. "Because Turkey may be a despised nation," said Mr. Stafford, "it is no reason why our government should tinge its own policy by becoming a party to the difficulties existing between Turkey and Greece . . . Better far to keep aloof from participation in the difficulties that confront the Balkan States than to make a good bargain with a nation hard pressed for ships of war." Many more hours of warm debate passed before the vote could at last be taken, when the Naval Appropriation Bill was passed by 174 votes to 87, the price being $11½m, more than enough for a brand new super-Dreadnought for the U.S. Navy. "This is," commented Secretary Daniels, "a splendid thing for the Navy."

The Greeks thought it a splendid thing for their navy, too, though Admiral Mark Kerr, still in office, still hankering after a fleet air arm rather than battleships, submarines rather than battle cruisers, described these second-hand purchases as "useless, worn-out, and obsolete battleships, which could neither steam nor effectively use their nearly worn-out guns." Nobody listened to the English Admiral, least of all Prime Minister Venizelos, who now took no notice of his Commander-in-Chief. In Athens and everywhere in Greece there was jubilation at the news of the American Congress's decision. At last, they believed, they had in their possession the power to reply to the guns of the big battleship when she arrived from England.

There was a widespread belief—in Washington, London and Paris as well as Athens—that "the danger of an immediate outbreak, at least, has been postponed," as the *Daily Telegraph* expressed it. There was to be no delay in the delivery of the two vessels, now renamed *Kilkis* and *Lemnos,* and they would be handed over complete with supplies and provisions, coal and ammunition. The *Idaho,* conveniently already in Europe, was to steam from Malta to Gravesend, where her crew were to be taken off by the U.S.S. *Alabama,* and be replaced by her Greek crew, already *en route* for England. The *Mississippi* was at Pensacola, and was directed to sail for Boston, where a similar transfer of crews was to take place. The two vessels would then sail—as early as mid-

July, it was hoped—for Athens. If there were no hitches, it was thought possible that they could be in the Piraeus just before the *Sultan Osman I* arrived in the Golden Horn, but it was evidently going to be a close-run race.

CHAPTER FOUR

The Turkish Sailors

The last Brazilians had left Tyneside in 1913 before the winter set in. Their departure was mainly lamented. There were few regrets about the absence of the fifty lower grade technicians who had lived at Tower House on Quay Side, and over the last months had turned it into a bawdy house and caused a heavy increase in the spread of venereal disease in the city. But the supervisors, of whom there were more than a hundred, had remained respectable and well-liked, and their rents had brought real comfort to many homes where they lodged. By October they had all gone, except one, Senor Lopez, who especially fancied Newcastle, had married a local girl and opened up a small grocery business, which flourished.

Many of Armstrong's men who had been working on the battleship were offered other work, for the yard had got their contract for another British super-Dreadnought. Others remained unemployed, and there was a touch of depression again at Elswick in the weeks before Christmas. As always, it was the unskilled labourers who were worst hit. They were traditionally treated with little consideration, and with a rate of pay, when they were working, of only 18s. a week—half that of a tradesman—any sort of saving against a rainy day was out of the question. As the days became colder, more bare-foot children were to be seen outside Armstrong's gates, and at the entrance to the tunnel that ran under the Scotswood Road into the works, when shifts were changed

—even at 6 o'clock in the morning. And their cries of "Any bread left? Any bread left?" to the men as they hurried home with their dinner boxes, that were nearly always empty, became more pleading. It looked like being another bad winter.

The big battleship, occupying nearly seven hundred feet of the quayside, lay like a grey gaunt derelict, her decks littered with steel plates and derricks, boxes of rivets and ladders and a multitude of anonymous and abandoned interior and exterior fittings. With the coming of the November rains she began to assume a deep red hue, and in the shipyard she was unofficially, inevitably, and without bitterness, re-named H.M.S. *Rust*. A few of her guns had been fitted, in a haphazard, unthreatening sort of way, it seemed: they only added to her appearance of forlorn cheerlessness. For the present she was still the biggest, and also the least dangerous-looking, battleship in the world. It seemed unlikely that anyone could ever want her again.

Then, on the first day of the New Year, the men who had, months before, been working on the battleship were surprised to see in their local newspaper an imaginative drawing of her as she would appear when completed. Now she was flying the Turkish flag, and set into the picture was a photograph of "Captain Raouf, of Turkey, who is in London in connection with the matter". "This dramatic purchase," as it was described, had been accompanied by some very quick work by the press department of the Turkish Embassy in London.

The news that someone had bought this sad great vessel, and for nearly three million pounds, came as a complete surprise to Newcastle. Once again, and again inexplicably, this was to be a rush job. By the middle of January, 1914, joiners, plumbers, electricians, shipwrights and many other tradesmen were being signed on for work on the big battleship, now more formally and more grandly known as "the Sultan". And there was to be every opportunity for overtime. Work was renewed towards the end of the month, in bitter

weather. To those who were first to board the battleship
after her four months of stagnation the overwhelming impression was of dirtiness. Inside and out she was filthy. "I've
never seen such a mess. Everything was inches deep in dust
and rust," a plumber's mate remembers. "It took days to
clean her up."

The Turks arrived at the end of the month. There had
never been Turks in any numbers in Newcastle before, and
they made a colourful and lasting impression. The officers
were the first to arrive, very dark, very correct and very
clean, wearing dark blue suits and fezzes, although one had
an astrakhan hat as protection against the east wind. They
found themselves pleasant rooms outside the city, at the
Manor House Hotel in the prim seaside resort of Whitley Bay
just north of the estuary of the River Tyne. Armstrongs
found this advance party offices in a house standing alone
in a field near their Scotswood works, and an office boy to
attend to their small material needs. His name was Stan
Johnston, and he was then a 14-year-old apprentice with keen
ambitions and an eye for the main chance. "I well remember
Captain Hassan, a tall very quiet officer, and Lieutenant
Arrif, Lieutenant Mazmi and the other Turkish gentlemen,
none of whom could speak a word of English. At this time
I was browsing round the second-hand bookshops for text
books, and in Robinson's bookstall in the Butcher Market I
came upon a Turkish-English lexicon. It was priced at fifteen
shillings—much more than I could afford. After borrowing
from my sisters, I duly became the proud possessor of this
text which I took to the office the following Monday."
Young Johnston's duties were only to keep the offices clean,
to refill the inkwells and replace the blotting paper. He was
properly tipped for these minor services. But "armed with
this dictionary, which was complete with phrases—very useful—I made myself absolutely indispensable to these Turkish
gentlemen, and there was seldom a week that the remunera-
tion was less than seven to ten golden sovereigns"—five times
the wage of a skilled tradesman. Johnston became the trusted

confidant of these Turks, translating technical terms so that these could be made clear to Armstrong's officials, and at weekends when they disappeared to London for an evening out, he would occupy their rooms at their hotel as their only protection, they considered, against the loss of their personal possessions.

In apparent contradiction to the appeals for urgency from Constantinople and the Turkish naval attaché in London with which Armstrongs were bombarded, these officers worked at a leisurely tempo and with the same cultivated absence of zeal which Admiral Kerr had reported on ten years earlier. They arrived at their office, itself separated by some miles from the dirt and the clamour of their battleship, at ten in the morning, drove into Newcastle for a leisurely lunch at one of the hotels, and had left for the day by three in the afternoon. Apparently satisfied with the fighting prowess of their vessel, they were preoccupied with its creature comforts rather than its guns. They were happy to discover that in this respect Brazilian naval tradition was cast in the same mould as their own. A ship was for living in often for weeks or months at a time; a battle was a brief business by comparison. By its very nature, a man-of-war made an uncomfortable home, but at least the Brazilians had recognized that a ship of vast dimensions not only intimidated the foe, it also offered a splendid spaciousness in its accommodation. Below decks "she was like a town", as one of the 150 plumbers working on her at this time reported. Her seamen's flats spread almost ninety feet across the full width of the ship, and the petty officers were provided with individual partitioned cabins and bunks, a rare luxury. The half-deck was enormous, and forward of it was the officers' wardroom, theatre-like in its appearance and dimensions of some eighty-five by sixty feet. Abaft the half-deck were the admiral's quarters, comprising a large dining-room, a day cabin and two sleeping cabins—one for a distinguished guest. An admiral's walk was already provided for: which was just what the Turks would have asked for anyway. The officers' cabin flats, below the admiral's quarters, were just like those in a cruise liner, one for each officer, with opening scuttles for daylight. The ship's galleys, the showers and bathrooms, her recreational equipment, had all been laid out for comfortable living and convenience, and above all to offer a sense of space and freedom. This had been achieved by eliminating from the design all possible watertight bulkheads that might limit the size of the compartments and interfere with the crew's comfortable and natural progression about the ship.

The layout met the Turkish ideal in every respect, so that the delegation could give their mind to the choice of wood to complete the panelling, the style of the three-piece electric lamp fittings, armchairs, desks and tables for the wardroom, and the furnishings for the admiral's quarters, which were to be the *pièce de résistance*. By March there was a record number of joiners at work on the battleship, fitting the mahogany panelling prepared ashore by the cabinet makers in the carpenters' shops. Much of the work called for special timber and special skill with beautiful veneers for the detail work. Carefully seasoned Honduras mahogany was used for many of the fittings, and nine-foot lengths of it for the admiral's sideboard which was secured across the width of the dining cabin at the extreme stern. The fitted bevelled framework round the ports, too, de-manded specialized skills; even the securing mouldings for the wall panelling were of an elaborate design. By this time more Turkish supervisors had arrived—"very respectable they were, too," one joiner remembers them, dressed in tidy blue overalls and the inevitable fez, "calling everyone 'Effendi' and hustling us along politely but getting in the way all the time."

For some six months the big battleship again provided Newcastle upon Tyne with an ever-growing spectacle of wonder and an inexhaustible topic of conversation. Her suc-cessful launching had properly crowned this first phase in her career. Before her completion and her trials there remained to be played out an entr'acte which was enjoyed by almost as many of Newcastle's citizens as the launching itself. In order to complete her fitting out, the *Sultan Osman I* had to pass down the river from the Elswick yard to the new Armstrong yard at Walker. On a bleak rainy day in June, 1914, the big battleship cast off from her Elswick quayside, and steaming under her own power for the first time and with black smoke pouring from her two wide-spaced funnels, she nosed out into mid-river, the biggest warship ever to sail down the Tyne. Many of the men who were still working on her were on board for the journey, many more lined the river banks, calling out and waving, and sirens sounded from the moored vessels as she steamed slowly and magnificently past them, nursed gently along by a pair of tugs. To those standing on Redheugh Bridge, the first under which she passed, she presented a curious as well as an overwhelmingly impressive sight as she approached. Some of her big guns were mounted, in other of her turrets there were only black cavities. Amidships she was a shambles of half completed upperworks, and her twin flying bridges linking her funnels and spanning her two amidships turrets—nicknamed her "Marble Arch" —was a confusion of steel framing, and her fore bridge was a mere skeleton of steel uprights and ladders. The inadequate clearance of Newcastle's bridges had made it necessary to hinge both tripod foremast and mainmast, and the upper halves were folded flat and supported on temporary struts. " 'The giant' looked a mess that day," one eyewitness remembers. "But she was big all right." Her bulk and length seemed to enlarge as the river narrowed and the banks closed in slightly about her just above the bridge. She slipped under at less than one knot, taking an interminable time, her funnels seeming to come perilously close to the under part. The two railway bridges, the King Edward VII and the High Level, gave no cause for anxiety. But it seemed hardly possible that she could ever squeeze between the piers of the Swing Bridge below. Smaller

vessels than the *Sultan Osman I* had been in trouble here
in the past, and the fire brigade was out with hoses at the
ready in case the friction of her hull against the wooden
protective buffers should cause a fire. But this hazard, too,
was safely negotiated at a scarcely perceptible speed and to
the disappointment of a large number of small boys, the
ship berthed safely at the new Walker yard in the late
afternoon. Here her interior and external fittings would be
completed, her remaining guns hoisted aboard, her magazines filled with ammunition. Then, after her trials, she
would be ready to sail with her first crew down the North
Sea and Channel, through the Mediterranean and the
Aegean Sea itself, which she was to dominate by her size,
her awesome reputation, and the power of her 12-inch guns.

Now the men had to travel down river daily from Elswick. Even in summer this could be a cold business, and it
made for greater hustle than ever. The company's launches,
the *Winifred* and *Armstrong,* cast off at 6.05 a.m., on the
dot, and it was just that much more of a run from the
"British Lion" and the other pubs along Scotswood Road
to the quayside. As the summer advanced, the sense of
urgency became more marked. Still more men were transferred to the *Sultan Osman,* and Armstrongs had to commission boats from the General Ferry Company to take
them to and from the Walker yard. By late June, with only
a few days left before she was due to leave for her trials,
there were more than a thousand men at work from before
seven to five-thirty in the evening, when the night shift took
over. There was no pause at week-ends. She had become
as clamorously alive as she had been when the Brazilians
had been pressing so hard and anxiously for an accelerated
delivery time.

Among the alterations that had to be carried out were
those demanded by national custom and tradition. Some of
these took priority over attention to the ship's military readiness in this race against time, and the arrival of the American battleships in Greece. Turkish naval tradition, for ex-

ample, obliged the engineer officers to be socially separated from their fellows. This division dated back to the earliest days of steam in most navies, but the class distinction, even in the British service, did not go to the lengths practised in the Ottoman Navy. Not only were the engineer officers' cabins properly separated, but an annexe had to be partitioned off in the ward room so that these oil-stained machinery men would not sit with their fellows, nor of course eat with them, for in the Turkish navy it had always been accepted that engineer officers ate with their fingers and required no silver or cutlery.

Then there was the matter of the plumbing. The baths and showers, varying from public for the men to tiled privacy for the officers and a fully-equipped, fully-tiled suite for the admiral, required only minor modification, although the brass fittings were replaced by the latest electroplated taps and Watsonian mixers, and all the taps had to be lowered so that feet, hands and faces could be washed in the oriental manner. But oriental custom also demanded elaborate changes in the lavatory arrangements. All the water closets—for a ship's company of 1,100 officers and men, and fitted only during the previous summer—had to be unscrewed, disconnected and replaced by some one hundred and fifty Moslem bowls, for the convenience of "the Turkish squatters" as Tyneside ribaldry dubbed them. These consisted of inverted cones sunk into the deck and flanked by foot-plates, and placed in two long open facing rows in the seamen's heads. Those for the petty officers were separated by sheet iron divisions, with cold water taps conveniently placed for the left hand—the men were supposed to bring their own water in tin cans; while the officers were provided with doors with locks and pink fully-tiled walls and floors.

By this time, now that it was believed that the Greeks would be taking delivery of their American battleships the following month, the pressure on Armstrongs became more severe. Captain Raouf Bey had arrived from Turkey. He and his senior officers were residing in a hotel in Newcastle, and every day drove down to Walker to hustle things along. In contrast with the officers of the advance party, Raouf was more concerned with the fighting prowess of his vessel and this now received more attention. Some of the secondary armament of 6-inch and 3-inch guns was complete and mounted, but the delivery of a number of her 6-inch and the last 12-inch weapons had been delayed. Twelve of these big guns were almost ready, and most of these had been fitted by mid-June. But two of them were still being proved, it was said, and there was a succession of hold-ups with the new hydraulic controller, which promised well but because of its radical design was causing further delay. Armstrongs reassured their clients that all would be well, and increased still further their labour force. In an effort to prevent absenteeism during race week, traditionally held in the last week in June, special arrangements were made. "Pressure is being used by the builders to complete the vessel," reported *The Shipbuilder,* "which is required to be docked by 11th July. Workmen have been engaged at the Scotswood, Elswick and Walker works of the company during the whole of the Newcastle Race Week holidays. At the former establishment, where the ammunition is being prepared, men have been paid at the rate of time-and-a-quarter, and the same arrangement has been in operation at the ordnance department, where the gun sights are being completed. At Walker, where the vessel is completing, the joiners and carpenters have received a bonus of 10s. each for the race week over and above their time-and-a-half rates." "I couldn't keep my eyes open when I got home those nights," one joiner recalls today.

Armstrongs were certainly putting on a great show of energy and willingness. At the end of June they told Raouf that the extreme measures had had their effect, that his battleship would be ready by July 7th, four days earlier than scheduled, and before the ex-U.S. Navy battleships could leave for Greece. She would lack only some of her

6-inch and two of her big guns, her gunsights and ammunition. But of course her trials also still remained to be
carried out. To meet the terms of their contract with the
Ottoman Navy she must go through the formal tests for
seaworthiness. Her engines remained to be tested for power
output and consumption, her steering gear, her complex
communications system—a whole multitude of equipment
and fittings had to be searchingly tested. And she required
to be dry-docked, of course, after her long period in the
water. This would have to be done at Devonport, unfortunately one of the most distant bases in Britain from Newcastle.

Raouf Orbay fretted at the delay, but recognized its inevitability. In any case the *Sultan Osman*'s crew were not
due to arrive from Turkey until the last week of the month.
It was less easy to explain and forgive the continuing absence of two of the ship's main guns, those for number five
turret, which meant that her gun trials, which could have
been conducted during her journey to and from Devonport,
would now have to be carried out after her return. Raouf
proposed that, to save further delay, these trials could be
dispensed with. To fire her main armament on the way to
Turkey would provide her inexperienced gunners with
needed practice—perhaps practice against Greece's new
battleships *en route* to the Aegean.

There was little evidence at Armstrongs of deliberate
delaying tactics. Quite the reverse. Down at Walker there
was a record number of men at work on the ship, and
after dark the lights shone down on to her deck to speed
the work of the night shift. And yet among the more
curious of the men a few questions were being asked. At the
ordnance shop, for instance, the last two guns were ready,
now satisfactorily proved, ready for installation. And all
the gunsights had been completed. Why, one or two men
were asking, weren't they being fitted? On board the
Sultan Osman I they were trying to get the "tallies" changed
in time—these were the brass instruction and direction plates

for the communications, electrical, hydraulic, and ordnance equipment: hundreds of them scattered through the vessel. These had originally been etched in Portuguese, and were nearly complete when the Brazilians had abandoned her. Now they all had to be changed to Turkish tallies. This work was going ahead apace, but among those carrying it out there was some curiosity to know why on the reverse of every plate there was a translation of the text into English.

In spite of these setbacks, by the end of June the *Sultan Osman I* appeared to justify her name, and seemed worthy of all the adjectival enthusiasm which had been heaped on her from the day of her conception in the Ministry of Marine's office in Rio de Janeiro more than three years earlier. Abaft her two forward superimposed turrets and armoured conning tower arose her great tripod mast containing her bridge, and rising high above her fine foretopmast. Her two funnels, beautifully proportioned and widely spaced to add to her appearance of dignity and aggressiveness, were separated by two more twin 12-inch turrets, less in evidence for being secreted beneath the battleship's distinctive flying bridges. Abaft her second funnel arose her after superstructure, bristling with more guns, and her tripod mainmast: and then her enormous quarterdeck dominated by three more 12-inch turrets, the centre turret rising above the other two. Even with two of her guns still absent, she offered an overwhelmingly handsome aspect: an impression of lordly arrogance combined with pugnaciousness—a credit to her builders, and to the unique talents of Eustace Hugh Tennyson d'Eyncourt.

On July 7th, 1914, in blazing sunshine, manned by a civilian crew and a scattering of Turkish technicians, the *Sultan Osman I* was eased out from the quayside at Walker, and with black smoke pouring from her funnels, was drawn slowly down the Tyne by her tugs. The giant was off on her trials at last.

*　　*　　*

The purchase of the big battleship by Turkey had had a galvanizing effect not only on the Ottoman Navy, but on the nation's morale. National celebrations followed the news that the Turkish treasury had beaten the Greek treasury in the race for money. Patriotic meetings presided over by officers of the Donanma Cemiyeti—the Turkish Navy League—were held in the big towns. After the frustrations and humiliations of two wars, the new battleship was regarded as a panacea for all the nation's troubles and injuries. The battleship, this biggest ever super-Dreadnought, built by the English—who ruled the waves and possessed the greatest empire—was now theirs, would blow to pieces the hated Greeks, would reclaim for Islam the territories lost in the recent wars. For a nation whose self-esteem was at the lowest ebb since the defeat by Russia in 1878, whose armies had more recently been routed by the Italians, the Montenegrins, the Serbs, the Bulgarians and Greeks, the navy became the rallying point, the object of possessive pride, of the Turkish people. At least there had been no grand defeat at sea, and the naval war had thrown up one real hero. And now the Treasury and the Ministry of Marine had provided the service with the weapon it most needed, a super-battleship unmatched by any other in the world. And she was to be under the command of the great Raouf Bey himself.

Meanwhile, the Turkish government was faced with a heavy burden. Payments for the battleship *Reshadieh* completing at Barrow-in-Furness were stretching to the utmost the resources of the Turkish treasury. There remained the problem of how to repay the short-term loan from the Perrier Bank. A sum of almost two and three-quarter million pounds was an appalling amount to find after a couple of expensive wars, and it was certainly not in the Ottoman treasury. And a secondary loan appeared to be out of the question. Talaat Bey, the Minister of the Interior, got down to some hard figures. There was a quarter million pounds of revenue to come from the annual sheep tax, and the

4

Ottoman Bank was willing to advance this sum on the security of this wool; it was, after all, indisputably there, up in the hills. A fund known as the public debt was worth £100,000, and the tobacco tax was good for another £50,000. The civil service and municipal functionaries of all kinds, and the officers of the army and navy, were as always on these occasions ripe game. Parliament therefore passed a law in late January 1914 authorizing the expropriation of all December salaries and wages, which had not been paid since September anyway. An agency report at the same time spoke of these civil servants "asserting their determination to forego another month's pay". Patriotism could scarcely go further. In Constantinople Talaat Bey convened a meeting of the municipality to discuss fund-raising projects, at which it was decided to introduce a bread tax of five paras on an oke, or a farthing on every 2¾-pound loaf.

By the end of January, 1914, nothing less than a great battleship-fund-raising crusade had gathered momentum under the enthusiastic impetus of Talaat Bey and the extremist patriotic elements of the Committee of Union and Progress and the Donanma Cemiyeti. There were street collections in Constantinople and all the larger towns of Turkey, boxes marked "For our Fleet" were rattled through the bazaars and the markets of towns and villages, and on the small ferry boats that plied the Bosporus. There were house to house collections, and women sold their hair "for our Fleet". Foreign government employees were given the option of declining to forego their salaries, but Egyptian and Indian Moslems in the country were soon drawn into the storm of maritime excitement that was sweeping the country. By April £450,000 had been collected, almost all of it in small contributions of a few paras or piastres. This was splendid progress indeed, although there was a setback when the treasury was forced to extract £60,000 from this sum to meet current expenditure. The newspapers reported no waning in the great enthusiasm at fund-raising public meetings, especially in Turkey's maritime provinces, and one correspondent in Constantinople wrote of the trials of rich individuals who became special targets in the campaign. Pamphlets were published and distributed in public places by the Committee of Union and Progress attacking and demanding £300,000 each from Chazi Mukhtar Pasha and Kutchuk Said Pasha, both ex-Grand Viziers who were notorious for their wealth and their past corrupt regimes.

The campaign to pay for the big battleship began to assume a spiritual character that served to unite the country more closely than the late wars had ever done. "The national attention seems for the moment to be entirely directed towards the fleet," reported *The Times* correspondent in Constantinople late in January. "Subscriptions continue to be collected in the provinces. The enthusiasm shown by all classes under the influence of stirring pamphlets and newspaper articles and theatrical performances appears to have greatly delighted the Grand Vizier and has encouraged the advocates of a large navy to urge the purchase of another super-Dreadnought." Now impelled to maritime excesses beyond those of the South American republics a few years earlier, the Ministry of Marine even opened negotiations with the builders of the *Rashadieh* for the renewal of work on her sister-ship, which had never got beyond the keel-laying stage before the Balkan War had caused work on both ships to be delayed.

Greece and Turkey had within twelve months therefore committed themselves to an expenditure of some £15m (say seventy-five millions in modern money or nearly half their total annual combined national revenue) on battleship construction and purchase, and half as much again on providing adequate fortified bases and docks for their new fleets.

The national campaign to pay for Turkey's big battleship may have produced an unprecedented enthusiasm for the Ottoman Navy among the common people of the Turkish

Empire, but scarcely one third its cost in hard cash. Through the early months of 1914 the problem of repayment of this loan continued to plague the officials of the Ottoman Treasury. Efforts to acquire a second and more substantial loan which would allow the country some working capital for the current year were renewed and carried on continuously in Europe's banking centres. The negotiators could reasonably claim that if there was to be another war against Greece, at least this time, with their overwhelming naval strength, they were certain to prove the victors. Then in April favourable word came back—again from France— about progress. The Grand Vizier at once despatched a minister to Berlin to bring to an end the negotiations there, and thence to Paris. Here he completed the work of his financial officers, and it was triumphantly announced that a £32m loan had been agreed, the first instalment payable on April 24th, and the balance later in the year. After liquidating their floating debt the Turkish government was left with a balance of £4,800,000 from this first instalment, which was used to settle claims for back pay among the civil servants and civilian contractors and £400,000 was voted to an urgently needed railway line. That left enough not only for Armstrongs' next instalment, but for the entire outstanding balance for the big battleship.

There remained the problem of finding a crew to man her. The *Sultan Osman I* would require a ship's company of about 1,100 officers and men, many of them trained in the modern specialized skills of wireless telegraphy, signalling, navigation and gun-laying. Even a stoker's job called for more than brawn. Since 1909 when Admiral Sir Douglas Gamble had first arrived in Constantinople to head the British Naval Mission to Turkey, he and his subordinates had been struggling manfully to bring about some sort of organization to the anarchistic administration of the Ottoman Navy and to improve the quality of its personnel, as well as to modernize the *matériel*. At all levels, in all departments, this was uphill work. The Moslem character did not take readily to filing, discipline, clean uniforms, inventories, inspections, stores and the Western accepted principles of law and order. *Laissez-faire* and corruption were the chief enemies. After struggling to obtain vital equipment, it often disappeared in a flash to the highest bazaar bidder. Gun sights and all optical equipment fetched high prices, and any form of firearm seemed to melt away before it could reach the armoury. Only a durable sense of humour saved these British officers from insanity. Admiral Gamble had been replaced by Admiral H. P. Williams, who in turn was succeeded in 1913 by Rear-Admiral A. H. Limpus, a meticulous, conscientious worker, a man of great charm, to whom the Moslem mind remained an enigma for the full term of his office. He found comfort in smoking very large cigars all day long, even in his bath. Admiral Limpus was assisted by six junior officers seconded from the Royal Navy, each a specialist in his own branch, and some sixty petty officers and ratings. Theirs was a curious assignment. They were subject to Ottoman Navy discipline, such as it was, and yet were regarded as a cut or two above their Turkish brother officers and were given inflated ranks, a Royal Navy lieutenant becoming a Corvette Captain, with the courtesy title of "Bey" after his name. They wore elaborate Turkish rig with outsize epaulettes and gold distinction lace and aiguilettes of gold cord, and the traditional fez at all times.

In the latter part of 1913, the training of the crew for the smaller battleship *Reshadieh* was well in hand. The problems of giving the men a superficial knowledge of the working of a modern battleship were at least on their way to solution, although it had been a formidable and exasperating task. On December 29th the Minister of Marine called for Admiral Limpus. "Well, Admiral, we have two Dreadnoughts now," Djemal Pasha told him in tones of extreme satisfaction. "This new one is much bigger and more powerful. We must now train a crew for her and there is not much time. You have the whole navy to choose from, and I give you a free hand to pick the officers and crew from the whole fleet."

No purpose was served in pointing out that there was almost no one left to pick and choose from. Conscription in the Turkish navy worked in a five-year cycle, with one fifth of the total personnel released every year. The Italian and Balkan wars had quite disrupted this orderly scheme and many of the men had not seen their homes for eight or nine years. Grumbling had recently deteriorated into rest-lessness and insubordination. There had been several full-scale mutinies in the antiquated hulks anchored in the Golden Horn. The best officers and the reliable men were already earmarked for the *Reshadieh*. There was no question of drawing the *Sultan Osman*'s crew "from the whole fleet". The only answer to the problem was to conscript them from the fishing villages of the maritime provinces. The balance was made up of peasants from villages up in the hills: some five hundred in all, barely half the number required, but sufficient for a skeleton crew. It was hoped that additional men could be found, technically trained for their tasks, from among the civilian dockyard men working at Armstrongs, and the Royal Navy promised to provide some pensioned-off petty officers who might be glad of the money and the chance to serve afloat again.

In addition to the Training Station on the island of Halki, a Naval Training School was set up in the Sultan's palace, and here the British officers set about introducing illiterate peasants and fishermen into the secrets of longitude and latitude and the observation of celestial bodies, the purpose of boiler element economizers and the function of double-ported slide valves, and the importance of the balance chamber in the Whitehead torpedo. Above all, gun crews had to be trained how to load, lay and fire the *Sultan Osman*'s 12-inch, 6-inch and 3-inch guns. A nucleus of gunnery officers were despatched to Britain, where they were given a rush course at Whale Island, the Royal Navy's gunnery establishment. At Whale Island there were installed for their instruction twin 12-inch dummy guns in turrets similar to the *Sultan Osman*'s. It was a trying experience for these officers, for they had not been paid for some time and their clothes were the worse for wear. They ordered fresh uniforms on credit from Gieves the famous naval outfitters of Portsmouth, and when it was time for them to leave, their debts unhonoured, there was trouble with the local police. True to tradition, their British fellow naval officers passed round the hat and settled their substantial account without demur.

In Constantinople, the main task of training the gun crews was in the hands of Corvette Captain Frank Elliott Bey, the British Naval Mission's Gunnery Adviser. Captain Elliott's difficulties were formidable, for he was almost entirely without equipment to instruct his eager new recruits. Firstly, he required a ship, with guns. The old *Messudiyeh* appeared to be ideal for his purpose. She was an ancient ironclad battleship of 10,000 tons, armed with 9.2-inch and 6-inch guns of such an age that even the antiquated Turkish fleet had not required her for active duties. Captain Elliott inspected her, found her rat-ridden and filthier than any vessel he had seen in spite of service of more than two years with the Turkish navy; and then, before he could gain possession of her the Ministry of Marine decided she was past redemption, sent her heavy guns away to be re-lined (replacing them with wooden dummies to deceive the Greek spies), and took her light guns ashore and mounted them for the defence of the Dardanelles. Elliott finally succeeded in laying his hands on four antiquated pieces of field artillery, all of different calibres and of French, British, American and German origin, and went off in search of some ammunition. This, it seemed, had either been fired off in the recent wars, sold off to persons unknown, or was too dangerously old for use. Careful inquiry at last revealed that there might be a magazine store hidden away in an old mosque far up the Golden Horn. Some Turkish officers agreed to conduct him to it. At its entrance there was a danger sign, warning of the penalties exacted from those who entered carrying matches or wearing shoes. This seemed hopeful, and they entered. There were no lights inside, so to the dismay of Elliott the Turks in turn struck matches to show the way, and to reveal at last open tub after tub of damp powder, and long stacks of shells of all calibres, and all green with verdigris. "This is quite unsuitable for use," Elliott nervously informed his guides. "How can I teach my men gunnery with this?" The officers seemed offended at this reaction: this was, after all, an Aladdin's treasure house of high explosive. And in any case, it was all there was in the navy. So Elliott at length had it removed, the shells cleaned up, the powder carefully dried, and busied himself on his first course. He was given five weeks for each, and used as a target an old torpedo boat, the bare hull of which had survived twenty years of looting, and had this towed up and down off the island of Halki while his recruits shot at it. "They were a remarkable lot," Elliott commented. "Terribly enthusiastic, and patriotic—longing to do their bit. Few of them had even heard a rifle fired. And yet from the first round they never flinched. Even the toughest Royal Navy rating used to jump a bit at first." After each session the torpedo boat was pumped out and plugged and used again and again, until on one evening the plugs were forgotten, and the next day the torpedo boat was at the bottom. Elliott was furious and demanded a court martial; the Turkish officers were less concerned: "It's all right, she was insured," he was told.

All the British officers were daily exercising their ingenuity in overcoming obstructionism, inefficiency, lethargic officialdom and above all corruption. "It was fine training for all of us." And yet they were constantly being pressed to speed their training schedule. When word was received in Constantinople that the Greeks might be offered a pair of American battleships, the order went out to accelerate the programme. Elliott cut his gunnery course to three weeks, and that was not much for men who must soon handle the elaborate sighting and range mechanism, the revolutionary hydraulic loading gear of the *Sultan Osman*'s main 12-inch batteries. In April he managed to acquire the *Muin-i-Zaffer,* a coast defence vessel of greater antiquity than the *Messudiyeh* and dating back to the age of sail, although she had been somewhat rejuvenated more recently. Elliott stripped off most of her equipment and armament, and had secured to her decks his mixed battery of field artillery. At least with this, and the addition of a Vickers range clock and voice pipes, it was possible to simulate in miniature and in muted form what it would be like aboard the *Sultan Osman* when she began to annihilate the hated Greeks. The Minister of Marine liked to join Elliott aboard the *Muin-i-Zaffer* when there was a shoot on, to encourage the men, and remind Elliott of the need to hasten. The *Sultan Osman* would be ready in July, he was told. Already a transport, the *Neshid Pasha,* had been found to transport her crew to Newcastle. In a few weeks they would be sailing, leaving Turkish shores with a heroes' farewell.

The efforts of Admiral Limpus and his staff to pave the way to Ottoman triumph at sea were matched by the zeal of the German military mission in Constantinople to prepare the Turkish army for victory on land. For more than five years Turkey had been subjected to increasing political, economic and military pressure from Germany and Britain, and had found herself in turn cajoled, threatened, deprived and courted. British policy was curiously inconsistent. The British government on the one hand despised Turkish ineptitude and inefficiency, and on the other hand feared lest she should be drawn so closely into the German camp that she would become an active ally in war. Churchill as First Lord felt no confidence in the Turks, and the First Sea Lord, Prince Louis of Battenberg, wanted to withdraw

Admiral Limpus and his staff from Constantinople. The Foreign Office, on the other hand, saw the balance of power in the Mediterranean benefiting from an efficient modern Turkish navy, and the British government was quite happy to see the big battleship go to Turkey rather than Greece, while the Perrier Bank of Britain's closest ally financed the purchase.

There was no ambivalence in German policy towards Turkey. Without stealth or subtlety, a German military mission worked on an ever-increasing scale in Constantinople, equipping the army willy-nilly with Krupp guns, instructing them in the glories of German militarism and the wickedness of British imperialism. The man chiefly responsible for this renaissance was General Liman von Sanders, who took upon himself the title of Inspector-General of the Turkish Army. He and his Chief-of-Staff, von Strempfel, terrified the Turks by their arrogance, self-confidence and overbearing manner. These two were ably backed up by the German ambassador, Baron von Wangenheim. By 1914, the German efforts had brought about a transformation in the spirit and efficiency as well as the *matériel* of the Turkish army. One observer reported how "The troops round Constantinople were drilling constantly. This we put down then to the recognition of the bad figure they had cut in battle against the Bulgarians and Serbs, but now can recognize that the considerable increase of German officers was not induced merely by the fear of further struggle with any Balkan State . . . I found Turkish soldiers everywhere being carefully and thoroughly drilled. The Turkish soldier was no longer the lethargic creature that I had known for forty years in time of peace. The discipline was evidently stricter, and the officers in particular left the impression that they expected soon to be called upon to march."*

In their new arrogance, the Turkish army officers despised the navy men, and were jealous of their public popularity. There developed during the first half of 1914 a deep rift

* *Forty Years in Constantinople* by Sir Edwin Pears (1916).

between the two services, the Army and one section of the cabinet becoming enthusiastically pro-German while the Grand Vizier himself, Djemal Pasha and other cabinet ministers, and the officers of the Ministry of Marine and the navy remained loyal to the British cause, which was pressed modestly and without flamboyance by Admiral Limpus and his staff. If the pro-British clique had lost ground to the Germans over the past months of intensive army activity, there could be no doubt that the status and power of the navy—and of the British cause—would be immeasurably increased with the arrival of the *Sultan Osman I* in Turkish waters, and the victories she would at once achieve over the Greeks.

This clear-cut line between the two services and their loyalties to the two Great Powers was confused when the German navy sent into the Mediterranean a powerful and modern naval squadron headed by the brand new Dreadnought battle cruiser *Goeben*. This further upset the balance of maritime power in the Mediterranean, already made precarious by the construction of new Dreadnought fleets by Austria-Hungary and Italy. Another purpose of this move was to demonstrate, especially to the Turks, that Germany was mighty now not only on land but at sea as well. The *Goeben,* the most formidable battle cruiser in the world, made an impressive sight as a flag-shower. The British replied by sending into the Mediterranean a complete battle cruiser squadron, consisting of the *Inflexible* (flag), *Indomitable* and *Indefatigable* under the command of Admiral Sir Archibald Berkeley ("Arky-Barky") Milne, an amiable socialite, "an officer of inferior calibre, utterly lacking in vigour and imagination, whose appointment to the Mediterranean Command in 1912 had largely been due to Court influence."[*] These two rival squadrons cruised the Mediterranean competing in turn-out and seamanship, the arrival of the single shimmering white *Goeben* at Constan-

* From the *Dreadnought to Scapa Flow,* Vol. II, by Arthur C. Marder (1965).

tinople being followed by the equally showmanlike anchoring of the equally glittering British Dreadnoughts. Turkish tours of inspection of the German battle cruiser and of her 11-inch gun turrets were matched shortly after by invitations to parties of Turkish naval officers to inspect the British battle cruisers' 12-inch guns—with, let it be noted, their very up-to-date hydraulic loading system. The German commander, Rear-Admiral Wilhelm Souchon, was as brilliant and formidable a commander as Milne was lethargic and incapable. Yet when the two flagships found themselves in the same port together, the customary friendly relationship between the German and British officers was always evidenced. Dinner invitations were exchanged. There were gay musical evenings, and the officers came to call each other by their Christian names. It was all most pleasant and peaceable, and in most marked contrast with the tense relationship between Admiral Limpus and General von Sanders ashore.

By late May, 1914, Admiral Limpus and his harrassed staff had done all that time permitted to train the big battleship's scratch crew. These five hundred ratings, possessing a thin veneer of knowledge of their specialized trades but all the enthusiasm and lust for combat that Raouf Bey could ask for, were packed into the transport *Neshid Pasha* at Constantinople and cheered off down the Hellespont. It was a glorious occasion, a prelude, it was believed, to a glorious victory.

CHAPTER FIVE

The Seizure

In the harsh and uncertain world of shipbuilding the sea trials of a new ship offered the workmen a welcome bonus, a healthy break in routine, and a chance for a spree. There was always strong competition especially among the younger men for selection as dockyard crew for a ship's trials. The trials of the *Sultan Osman I* were looked forward to with specially keen anticipation, and not only because her size would require an unusually large complement of men. By this time a special loyalty as well as affection for the battleship had grown among the workmen. Her towering funnels and masts and superstructures, her great "Marble Arch" flying bridges, had come to be accepted as part of the city's skyline. The vicissitudes through which she had passed, shared by the workers' families, had served to increase the special regard in which she was held. It seemed odd to think how Tyneside would be without her.

The trials were a curious occasion, part celebratory feast, part technical exercise, part invigorating cruise on the briny. Some two hundred of the fortunate selected dockyard men, representing many trades, came aboard the battleship at the Walker yard, each with his wooden box of tools and his cheap fibre suitcase or kitbag of personal possessions, and established themselves uneasily in the *Sultan Osman*'s luxurious quarters like some workmen's delegation assigned to a five-star hotel for a Trades Union Conference. Most of the younger men had never before taken part in these proceedings and were at first self-conscious in their role of half-guest, half-artisan. They had brought aboard bottles of spirits and beer, and on their first evening many of them broke up into drinking parties with their mates. Late on that evening of July 7th as the big battleship steamed down the North Sea past the mouth of the Humber there was a good deal of light-hearted sport in the seamen's flats, and when eventually the hammocks were slung—sometimes with difficulty—and the men attempted to climb into them, the celebrations reached a jovial climax, many a stoker or electrician being tipped out on to the deck.

Standing aloof from these activities were the Turkish technicians, who completed the vessel's oddly mixed complement. By their religion they were prohibited from the consumption of alcohol, and, while they had witnessed some foreign and distressing sights on the street corners of Newcastle on a Saturday night, they had not before been placed in such close proximity to such un-Islamic festivities. On the following day they were relieved to find events taking a more practical turn, and to discover that the real purpose of this summer voyage was, after all, being carried out. The *Sultan Osman I* was under the command of a naval architect from Armstrong's design department, a man with much seagoing experience, Mr. Chalder Cutt. He had deputed responsibility for the discipline and good conduct of the men to Bill Palmer, a fierce fitter foreman, who made it clear that this was not going to be a prolonged drinking bout but a hard job of work. "You're being paid time-and-half for twenty-four hours a day," he told his men, "and I'll make you work for that time if I have to. There'll be a pint of beer at dinner and one at supper, and there'll be no more drinking than that." For the rest of the day the men went about their work, seriously and conscientiously, observed and followed at every step by the eager Turkish technicians, each in fez and blue working overalls. Some could speak a little English, and at work, where there were none of the differences of custom in religion, eating and recreation, the two races got on well, attention to practical matters being broken by light-hearted banter. In blazing summer sunshine on July 8th the *Sultan Osman I* steamed down Channel at cruising speed with the dockyard men working all day checking the voice pipes, the telephones, the cabin bells, the electrical circuits and fuses, the water pipes, the manual and hydraulic gun gear, the steam pressure and coal consumption, and the multitudinous components and instruments, the steam, electric and hydraulic power, the complex interdependent and interlinked webs of tubes, pipes and cables that ran from stem to stern and from masthead to the boiler rooms of the vessel. It was a long day's work for every man aboard and most of them slung their hammocks or took to their bunks early on the second night.

On the morning of July 9th they were off the red cliffs of Devonshire, with Dartmoor as a rising purple haze beyond. By midday they were in Plymouth Sound. Tugs came out to meet them, and they were towed slowly into Devonport dockyard, an object of special wonder and curiosity. Sightseers came out in boats, and the dockyard quays were lined with naval ratings and workmen. This Turkish giant was even longer than the newest British battleship they were building in the yard, and her seven turrets against the *Warspite*'s four gave evidence of a bristling and overwhelming fighting power. But two of her guns were missing, it was noticed—and that was unusual for a warship on her trials.

The *Sultan Osman I* went straight into dry dock for examination of her underwater fittings. She had been afloat for more than eighteen months, and stationary for almost all the time, so it was no surprise to find her bottom encrusted and filthy. The zinc protective plates over her brass valves were corroded almost through and spares had to be fitted while she was cleaned down. These were idle days for the stokers and many of the crew as well as the Turks. Most of the men had gone ashore on arrival. They were searched on leaving the ship, then escorted through the dockyard by a party of Royal Marines and left to find themselves lodgings in the city. During the day they wandered disconsolately round the streets, feeling as foreign and as far from home as the Turks themselves, dropping into strange pubs. In the evening there was more heavy drinking, especially among the trimmers and stokers. One was caught begging on a street corner, and others were locked up for the night and had to be bailed out by their mates the next morning. On the day they were due to leave they all had to be back on board by 6 a.m., and a sorry sight many of them made as they hurried up the gangplank, in no condition for the rigours of coaling ship that lay ahead. Later in the morning two colliers came alongside, and for six hours all hands had to take part in the filthy and back-breaking task of transferring some 1,500 tons of coal into the battleship's bunkers. In the evening all decks were washed down preparatory to sailing the following morning. No one was allowed ashore that night, but there was a good party below decks. A group of men had conspired with the crew of one of the colliers to hoist aboard a smuggled barrel of best Devonshire beer, disguised as a sack of coal. That night it was broached, and by midnight most of the men were drunker than they had ever been ashore in Plymouth's pubs.

The voyage home from Devonport was as calm and warm as the outward journey. Foreman Palmer was again in command of affairs, and it was a sober as well as a restful voyage. Most of the routine checking had been carried out, and the engineers and officers of Armstrong's design department were writing up their reports. One electrician remembers sunning himself all that first day at sea in a pinnace on the battleship's flying bridge, a telephone extension within reach in case he should be needed. That night as they passed off Spithead they witnessed a sight none of them would ever forget. King George V had been reviewing the British fleet. Some two hundred fighting ships had been drawn up in eleven lines—fifty-nine battleships, twenty-four of them Dreadnoughts, a total length of forty miles of men-of-war. The ships were lit overall, and hundreds of search-lights fingered upwards into the darkness and swung their beams to and fro in intricate patterns. It was a reminder to all those watching from the *Sultan Osman I* of the ultimate purpose of this great ship, and of all the specialized skill and materials that had gone into her construction. It was noticed after this event that the Turks became more impatient and fretful. After passing through the Dover Straits they constantly asked why they could not proceed at full speed all the way back to Tyneside. Why the delay? They must get back to Armstrongs, hoist in the last guns, the gun-sights and ammunition, and be on their way, for every day lost now was a gift to the Greeks.

The Greeks—the hated Greeks! Everywhere in the *Sultan Osman* their name could be heard, in Turkish and in English, spoken in venomous tones, with much spitting, by the Turkish technicians, and in comradely mimicry by the Geordie dockworkers. As the battleship steamed up the North Sea, the Turks could usually be found at the stern, leaning over the rail watching the white wake drifting away behind. Always the talk was of the Greeks—the dirty Greeks. Time and again the name was heard, like the obscenity that punctuated in tedious repetition the work-men's own everyday conversation, the battleship leaving astern along with its usual waste and kitchen litter, a trail of expectorated expletives. After an especially prolonged outburst it was seen that the Turks would turn and glance at the barrels of the four nearest 12-inch guns towering from the sixth and seventh turrets on the quarterdeck. There above them was the tangible evidence of power, the very weapons they needed to wreak vengeance on their enemy. This mighty ship would be theirs within a few days; all that they needed were the cordite and shells, and the sights to lay their guns.

On this homeward journey some of the Turkish officers approached the men in turn with the proposal that they should sail with them back to Turkey and take part as comrades in arms in the crushing victory over the Greek navy. It would be a wonderful experience, they were assured, something they would never forget. It would not be for long, and the pay was good—five times and more what they could earn in their trade—for the Ottoman Navy badly needed recruits with their skills. A small number of the ordnance, electrical and plumbing experts were to make up a skeleton crew to help sail the ship home, and many of these and others who thought it would make a bright summer holiday for them, agreed to sign on for three months. "We were all looking forward to it," said one plumber. "It was going to be a real lark."

The *Sultan Osman I* could not return directly to Tyneside, the Turks learnt. They had to pass the mouth of the Tyne and steam another eighty miles north to St. Abb's Head where the mile was measured out for her high speed trials. This news increased still further their impatience. The delays were mounting up to a frustrating degree. "How long will these take?" they asked, and were reassured when they heard that a day might suffice. And she was certainly a magnificent sight when the stokers worked her up to 19 and then to 20 knots, great gushers of black smoke pouring from her funnels, the bow wave climbing higher up the plating as the speed mounted, until the seas were coming over her forecastle. At 21 knots she seemed more than ever the embodiment of invincible power, her decks vibrating so that it was difficult to stand without support. She was doing over 22 knots as she entered the measured mile, her turbines putting out over 40,000 horsepower, and she was timed through at 22.42 knots, well above her designed speed. But then, thanks to Tennyson d'Eyncourt, and to Perrett's superb skill as a hull designer, Armstrong's ships always exceeded their contract figure. Further fuel consumption and turning trials followed, and the *Sultan Osman I* came through them all creditably.

No explanation was given either to the Turks or to the

dockyard crew why after the completion of the trials the battleship should steam north again. The men were not unduly anxious about this diversion because every day at sea added further to their pay packets. But the Turks were now bewildered and exceedingly anxious. The captain could only assure them that he was merely following orders, received from Armstrongs. On the evening of July 18th the battleship let go her anchors in the Forth just below the big railway bridge. That night a Scottish summer fog came down, enveloping the Forth and surrounding the battleship with a grey screen. It was still there the following morning, and the morning after, immobilizing the vessel. The men played cards, chatted together, wandered about in a state of boredom, and grumbled about the food. On the morning of the 21st, when the fog was thicker than ever, a picket boat was lowered and nosed its way cautiously into Leith harbour for much-needed provisions. That night there was a square meal for all, and on the following morning it was seen that the fog had cleared and that the battleship was surrounded by small boats which had put out on advertised excursions "to see the biggest battleship in the World". The whole estuary was alive with other shipping, too, released after three days of enforced idleness. Among the vessels was a large Hamburg-Amerika liner, packed with Germans who had been on a trip round the Scottish highlands, and whose tour had suddenly been cut short. Now they were on their way back home. Delayed newspapers told of a crisis. Austria-Hungary was close to war with Serbia. Archduke Francis Ferdinand, heir to the Austrian and Hungarian thrones, had been assassinated before the Turkish battleship had left on her trials, and the Newcastle newspapers had told of martial law in Sarajevo, student demonstrations, sharply-worded official demands and protests. With the lifting of that dark fog in the Forth there came news of preparations for mobilization, and of acute anxiety in Austria and Belgrade, St. Petersburg and Berlin, London and Paris.

At mid-day orders were given for anchors to be raised, the pleasure craft scattered, and in brilliant sunshine the battleship moved down the Forth, past Inchkieth and into the North Sea. At mid-day on July 22nd she steamed up the Tyne and once more tied up at the Walker yard "to receive her finishing touches prior to sailing for Turkish waters", as *The Shipbuilder* reported the occasion. Captain Raouf Bey was there to greet her, anxious and resentful at the delay, and commanding from Armstrong's officials the immediate fitting of her last guns, of her ammunition and her gunsights to make her ready for combat.

In the spring of 1914, the battleship race between Britain and Germany was approaching its climax. Over the past decade the lead had changed several times with the alternating alarms at future inferiority and the hasty completion of new vessels to redress the balance. Numerically the Royal Navy had never lost the advantage, but its maritime responsibilities extended over the trade routes of the world, and many other factors—the growing Dreadnought strength of Austria-Hungary and Italy among them—served to complicate still further the statistical permutations. In March 1914 Winston Churchill "claimed that he was maintaining the 60% standard of capital ship superiority which he had announced in March 1912, with a sufficient margin to meet requirements in more distant waters: 38–21 in March 1915, or five above 60%; 44–23 in March 1916, or eight above 60% . . ."* To the layman the interpretation of figures such as these was a bewildering task. For the politician they permitted any interpretation that supported their case, be it pacifist or extreme navalist. When Tirpitz publicly offered his readiness to accept a 16–10 ratio, in Britain's favour, the British Foreign Secretary retorted that "what Tirpitz said does not amount to much, and the reason for his saying it is not the love of our beautiful eyes, but the extra fifty

* *From the Dreadnought to Scapa Flow*, Vol. I.

millions required for increasing the German Army".

At the end of July the total Dreadnought strength of the Royal Navy in battleships and battle cruisers in Home waters was twenty-four. The German navy at this time could call on seventeen Dreadnoughts. This margin of superiority was far too slight for comfort, and it could be reduced to nothing perhaps by the temporary mechanical breakdown of several ships, or a series of misfortunes, from mine or torpedo, such as Japan had suffered in her recent war with Russia. In another year's time, with the completion of the huge programmes authorized in 1911 and 1912, the British navy would possess sufficient battleships to deter any attempt by the German High Seas Fleet to break out. Of the situation in the summer of 1914, Churchill has written, "There was not much margin here for mischance nor for the percentage of mechanical defects which in so large a Fleet had to be expected, and no margin whatever for a disaster occasioned by surprise had we been unready." Meanwhile there was a useful reserve of battleships nearing completion in British shipyards which could be drawn upon in an emergency. The Admiralty regarded the construction of foreign battleships in home yards as a form of war insurance: there were always clauses in the contracts giving Britain authority to take them over, with proper compensation, in critical circumstances. Churchill had been following with close interest and growing anxiety the progress of the last stages of completion of the Turkish battleships. Back in December 1913 he had favoured the sale of the *Rio de Janeiro* to Turkey: the Royal Navy did not want her, not in peace time; he was strongly in favour—unlike the First Sea Lord—of supporting to the utmost the efforts of Admiral Limpus in Constantinople; and he viewed the iminent arrival in Turkish waters of the big battleship as a gesture of defiance against Germany, whose political and military pressure on the Ottoman government was steadily increasing. But in Turkey there had been mighty changes since the big battleship had changed her name, and her final stages of construction had been accelerated. Disquieting reports had reached Churchill from Turkey of the ascendancy of the pro-German Young Turks who "looked towards Germany, and here they were very powerfully swayed by their military instincts and training. They rightly regarded Germany as the leading military power: many of them had received their military education in Berlin, and they were spellbound by the splendour and authority of Prussian organization".* As the political crisis of July 1914 deepened, Churchill "hoped for nothing" from Turkey, and "apprehended much". As always he saw developments and events in the widest view, but as First Lord his first concern was with preparations for a conflict at sea. He had no doubt that war in Europe was now imminent. "Our war arrangements comprised an elaborate scheme for dealing with vessels under construction . . . The plan of course covered all ships building in Great Britain for foreign powers . . . The Turkish battleships were vital for us. With a margin of only seven Dreadnoughts we could not afford to do without these two fine ships. Still less could we afford to see them fall into bad hands and used against us."*

As early as June the first hints had been dropped to Armstrongs by the Admiralty that it would be judicious to decelerate the last stages of construction of the *Sultan Osman I,* and the same suggestion had been made, again in strictest confidence, to Vickers, who were completing the *Reshadieh* at Barrow. Both companies were completely accustomed, by the nature of their business, to deal diplomatically with matters concerning defence policy. Thus, while Armstrongs put on a fine show of energy and speed, even having the *Sultan Osman I* ready four days early for her trials, no time could be spared for loading up her magazines, for fitting her gunsights, or her last guns, and in spite of the urgent pleas of her owners—and owners they

* *The World Crisis,* Vol. I, by Winston S. Churchill (1923)

THE SEIZURE   119

were, for the last cheque had now been paid—her trials
were conducted with painful care. (What was the delay of
a few days in order to get everything shipshape? A job
worth doing was worth doing well.)

But there was clearly a limit to the degree to which
Armstrongs could be asked to temporize; and this point was
reached by the arrival at Newcastle of the steamer *Neshid
Pasha* on July 27th. She steamed up the Tyne and tied up
in the Admiralty deepwater berth on the opposite side of
the river from the battleship. She was an insignificant, dirty,
single-funnelled vessel, more like a tramp steamer than a
trooper, an inappropriate conveyance for the crew of the
world's biggest battleship. But the spirit of eagerness of her
complement was evident from the moment she arrived,
and the Turks crowded on to deck, packing six deep against
the rails in an effort to catch a glimpse of their vessel.
Their journey in midsummer heat had been an arduous
one, but at last they were at their destination. Their own
maritime Mecca was there, hardly more than a cablelength
distant, as magnificently warlike and imposing as they had
been led to believe she would appear.

Now that he had his battleship back again at last, Raouf
Bey was hustling Armstrongs without restraint. He had
been given the date of August 2nd for final handing over,
and the Turkish flag was due to be hoisted at eight o'clock
on the following morning. The men had never worked
harder than in those last days of July putting the final
touches to the ship's fittings. One fitter remembers putting
in 15-hour days, with only three half-hour breaks, securing
the wire mesh guards round the exposed wheels of the valve
gear. Below decks, even with the fans full on, the heat was
almost unbearable. And all those who were there remember
seeing the Turks in their dirty steamer across the river,
packed tight on deck all day long, breaking off from their
distant surveillance only to offer prayers to Allah, their
intoning like a murmured chorus behind the crash of hammers and crane engines and the clatter of hob-nailed boots

on steel decks. "It was a pitiful sight seeing them there," one electrician recalls, "especially at the end when we knew there was going to be a war and they weren't going to get her."

On August 1st one of the *Sultan Osman*'s missing 12-inch guns was hoisted aboard from a floating crane which had brought them down river from Elswick, and the gunsights were also at last being secured. The last, the fourteenth gun was expected at any hour. But, to the irritation of the Turkish ratings and the fury of Raouf Bey, there was still no sign of the ship's ammunition—the hundreds of tons of 12-inch, 6-inch and 3-inch shells and their cordite propellent. It was maddening. It had, after all, been paid for.

None of the seamen from the *Neshid Pasha* had yet been allowed on board—nor had Raouf Bey allowed them ashore as their uniforms were no credit to their service, they were without money and he feared trouble—but the ship's petty officers and a small contingent of technicians frequently crossed the Tyne in their boat to inspect their ship and supervise the final stages. These Turks, and their fellow countrymen who had been lodging in the City for some weeks and had been on the ship's trials, were seen to be in a state of acute excitement during those last days, their impatience often obstructing the men and actually holding up completion of small jobs. The dockyard police had issued the Turks with passes to their own ship and were watching them carefully. There was a distinct feeling of tension in the ship. The nerves of both the workmen and the Turks were showing signs of fraying. All the light-hearted banter, the laughter over exchanged words and expressions in each other's language, had now ceased.

At the Admiralty, amid a multitude of problems requiring decisions during those last days of peace, the question of what to do about the *Sultan Osman I* and the *Reshadieh*

at Barrow was exercising Churchill's mind. He had heard
that the Turkish crew had arrived to take her over, that
Raouf Bey was pressing the builders for delivery. Raouf was
also known to be a wily politician, and on his showing in
the late war to be a brave and resourceful warrior. "There
seemed to be a great danger of the Turks coming on board,"
wrote Churchill of this situation, "brushing aside Messrs.
Armstrong's workmen and hoisting the Turkish flag." It
was more than a diplomatic embarrassment that Churchill
feared. Whether this ship escaped to Constantinople or Wil-
helmshaven the military result for Britain could be disas-
trous. As an enemy in the Mediterranean the battleship
might require weeks of hunting and a squadron to destroy
her, for a single enemy ship often demands the presence,
for hunting or pursuit, of three of four vessels of similar
power. As an additional unit in the German High Seas
Fleet, not only would the moral effect be considerable but
the delicate balance of Dreadnought strength would be
tipped still further against Britain. On July 31st, with the
delivery of a German ultimatum to France that must mean
war, Churchill drafted out a letter to Armstrongs. "As a
result of consultations with the Law Officers of the Crown,"
he wrote, "Messrs Armstrongs should be informed that they
must understand that in view of present circumstances, the
Government cannot permit the ship to be handed over to a
Foreign Power or to be commissioned as a public ship of a
Foreign Government, or to leave their jurisdiction."

On the morning of 1st August the Armstrong board con-
sulted with the local military, with the result that before
mid-day armed guards were posted at the gates to the dockyard. On the following morning, twenty-four hours before
the Turkish flag was due to be hoisted and she was to sail
for home, a company of Sherwood Foresters with fixed
bayonets marched through the dockyard and on to the ship.
Some of the Turkish officers aboard saw them coming,
and knew what it meant. There was no show of resistance,
and half an hour later every Turkish technician, petty officer

and officer on the *Sultan Osman I* had embarked in their boat for the last time, and were crossing the Tyne to the dirty little *Neshid Pasha*. They never glanced back at their ship.

CHAPTER SIX

The Pursuit

While at Newcastle during the last week of July and the first days of August 1914 the fate of the big battleship lay in the balance, her influence was already being felt in the Mediterranean, and in a theatre of war she was never to serve in. Her seizure by the First Lord on August 2nd was to have momentous results for both sides in the massive conflict that lay ahead. It was also to have a decisive and immediate effect on a pursuit and evasion that ran from Algeria to Turkey, and involved the reputations of a number of German and British senior naval officers, and of the British First Lord, Winston Churchill.

The chase of the *Goeben* serves as a remarkably apt illustration of the overall confusion which has dominated every long pursuit in naval history, of the fatal effects of timidity and indecision and of the decisive effects of enterprise and boldness. The naval position at the end of July was this. France had a force of mainly old warships to deal with the Austrian navy and possibly also with the navy of Italy, whose loyalties were uncertain. Austria and Italy now each possessed three Dreadnoughts. The Greek navy was about to be reinforced by two American battleships. The Turkish navy was due to be transformed into a major fighting force by the unexpected arrival of the modern Dreadnought *Reshadieh* and the great *Sultan Osman I* herself. Britain had a fleet of three battle cruisers, four armoured and four light cruisers, under Admiral Milne. Germany had the *Goeben* (Souchon) and her small and very fast cohort, *Breslau*. In the event of war Milne's first concern was to help the French ferry their colonial troops safely across the Mediterranean to Marseilles. His second obligation was to bottle up the Austrian navy in the Adriatic, and at the same time prevent Souchon from joining forces with his ally. And finally he was to prevent the escape of Admiral Souchon to the west, where his fast force could play havoc with Atlantic shipping.

Milne was from the beginning confused by the multiplicity of his tasks and uncertainty about their priority, torn by the contradictory nature of the signals he received from the Admiralty in London, and assailed by doubts about who was at war with whom, and when. He also had an inflated respect for his quarry, and for the fighting quality of the German ships, believing with good reason that his own ships were inferior if more numerous—a belief strongly confirmed by his second-in-command Rear-Admiral Sir Ernest Troubridge. Admiral Souchon was a man of decision, courage and political sagacity, whose force by its mere presence had for more than eighteen months contributed greatly to German political influence in the Mediterranean —above all in Turkey.

On July 28th, the day after the *Neshid Pasha* arrived in the Tyne with the *Sultan Osman I*'s crew, a number of events occurred that signalled the inevitability of a general conflict. Austria finally declared war on Serbia; the huge British First Fleet (soon to be properly renamed "Grand") was ordered to proceed to its war station at Scapa Flow; and negotiations were opened between Turkey and Germany on a secret alliance, the main clause of which obliged one party to come to the aid of the other in the event of war with Russia. Two days later, on July 30th, the two future naval antagonists in the Mediterranean were in their starting gates, Admiral Souchon coaling his ships at Brindisi, and Admiral Milne with his entire force—except one cruiser—370 miles away to the south-west at Malta. Souchon's orders were to interfere with the embarkation of French North African troops for France by bombarding the ports of Bône and Philippeville; Milne's orders from Churchill in London were, in the event of war, "to aid the French in the transportation of their African army by covering, and, if possible, bringing to action" Souchon's two fast ships. "Do not," ran the signal, "at this stage be brought to action against superior forces," except in combination with the French as part of a general battle. It would have appeared probable from these first instructions that an engagement between the two commanders was imminent, should war between Britain and Germany be declared. But here, even before the main pursuit of the crack German ships had begun, the ever-sensitive, ever-unpredictable time factor began to assert a domination of events that was to endure until the conclusion of the pursuit more than a week later. Milne had already been informed that war was probable and imminent. On the evening of August 3rd, he did not know the whereabouts of Souchon. In any case he would not have been allowed to engage him if he had found him, for while Germany and France were now at war, Germany and Britain were not. Nor could Milne, as a neutral, yet establish relations and communications on a war footing with the French commander-in-chief. For a commander unendowed with prescience or sagacity, it was an agonizing situation.

In short, Admiral Milne knew the position neither of his future friend nor of his future foe. From his base at Malta, the most central in the Mediterranean, Milne scattered his forces to all points of the compass in order to discover some news and prepare to meet his wartime commitments. To the north-east, to cover the entrance to the Adriatic, he sent Troubridge with his armoured cruisers and a flotilla of destroyers. The light cruiser *Gloucester* (Captain Howard Kelly) was later sent to watch the southern entrance to the Straits of Messina. Another light cruiser had sailed clear through the Messina Straits, reported them empty of the enemy and had been ordered back to base. Then he sent off two of his battle cruisers, the *Indomitable* and *Indefatigable*, to the west in case the French might need help. The French were, in fact, already on the way south from Toulon, under the command of the very able Admiral Boué de Lapeyrère, to escort the French troops across the Mediterranean. On the evening of August 3rd, then, the main body of all three forces, two at war and one still neutral, were heading for the same destination, the ports of Bône and Philippeville, the Germans with a head lead on their opponents.

During the night of 3rd–4th August, Souchon hourly expected orders from Germany directing his future movements. He knew that he could not remain for long at sea in the Mediterranean; his hunters were too numerous, his coal supplies too uncertain. He expected either to be sent back to Pola, where he would be safe behind the guns of this heavily fortified base, or back to Germany, after creating as much damage as possible to Atlantic trade on the way. The condition of his battle cruiser's boilers was also a cause for anxiety. The *Goeben* had been hustled out to the Mediterranean for political reasons before completing her trials, and she had not undergone a major refit since she had arrived more than a year and a half earlier. She had been due to be replaced by her sister ship, the *Moltke,* within a few weeks. But so poor was the state of the *Goeben*'s boiler tubes that, when war appeared imminent after the Sarajevo assassination, she had hastened to Pola where all hands worked in day and night shifts to replace her worn tubes with new ones rushed from Germany. Many of these had been dealt with when the inevitability of war became clear and she was ordered out of the Adriatic. The improvement in power of her engines was at once evident, and yet she was unable to sustain a speed higher than 18 knots, and could not approach the remarkable speed of 27.9 knots she was reported to have made on her trials.

At midnight Souchon's orders at last arrived by radio.

They came to him as a complete surprise. They were marked "of extreme urgency" and instructed him to make neither for Gibraltar nor Pola, but for Constantinople.

The reason behind this sudden change of plan lay in the development of negotiations in Constantinople between Enver Pasha, the Turkish Minister of War, and the German ambassador, von Wangenheim. The terms of the Treaty of Alliance between the two countries had been agreed and the German Chancellor had already telegraphed back a signed draft. The Turkish government was not prepared for such haste. Loyalties within the Cabinet were still in a state of conflict, and influences favouring neutrality under any circumstances remained powerful. Above all, the Grand Vizier "was fully alive to the precarious nature of his own position and to the fact that any real attempt on his part to run counter to the policy of Enver Pasha and the military authorities would have meant his elimination."* German pressure at this crucial moment was severe. The historic menace of the Russian bear to the east was again cited as a reason for establishing a protective link with the Central Powers; and with the inevitable triumph of Germany the Ottoman Empire, the Germans argued, would again be able to spread out to achieve her ancient and grandiose Pan-Islamic aspirations. Egypt, India and the other Moslem nations would be embraced by the power Germany could offer to Turkey. Such was the tone of German entreaties, already spiced with half-veiled threats of the consequences if the government refused to sign. Still the advocates of caution in Constantinople held out. Then on August 2nd came the news from England that Turkish naval officers had been driven off the *Sultan Osman I,* that British soldiers with fixed bayonets had established themselves on the battleship to forestall a threatened seizure by her Turkish crew, that the Turkish flag would now never be raised on the ship

* British Ambassador's Despatch, London, November 20, 1914.

which had become over the past months the symbol of the nation's new self-respect, and new power. Similar action, it was learnt, had been taken by the British with Turkey's second battleship. Overnight Turkey had been unscrupulously deprived of her new maritime power.

The effect of this unexpected and humiliating blow on the deliberations of the government and on the members with neutralist or pro-British sentiments was immediate. Djemal Pasha, the Minister of Maritime, friend of Admiral Limpus and of the other British Naval Mission officers, was struck with "mental anguish". For Enver Pasha it confirmed his worst judgements of the perfidy of Albion. And even the British ambassador later described the seizure as Turkey's "one concrete and substantial grievance against Great Britain". To the German government, fretting at Turkish delay and indecision, Churchill's action offered a heaven-sent opportunity for breaking once and for all the delaying tactics of the Turks and turning the key on the lock to seal off Russia from her allies. If the Turkish navy was to be deprived of her British-built Dreadnought—paid for by the Anatolian peasantry, by the very hair of the country's womenfolk, and ready to sail—then the least Germany could do was to offer her new ally the most powerful warship in the Mediterranean. Djemal Pasha was informed that the *Goeben* and *Breslau* were being re-routed to Constantinople, and was asked to permit their passage through the mine-fields and the Dardanelles forts. They would then be put at the disposal of the Turkish navy. At the same time, a signal was despatched to Admiral Souchon ordering him to turn east and steer for the Bosporus.

In the early hours of August 4th, the *Goeben* and *Breslau* continued on their westerly course. Souchon had interpreted his new orders to take effect after he had carried out his earlier instruction to attack the French transports expected to be now leaving Algeria. Before dawn he detached the

Breslau to deal with any French troopships at Bône with her 4.1-inch guns, while he steamed for Philippeville. At neither port was there any sign of the enemy, for Admiral de Lapeyrère, already proceeding at best speed from Toulon, had instructed the troopships to remain in convoy with him in view of reports that his adversary was making for Algeria. Souchon therefore had to be content with firing fifteen rounds of 11-inch shell at the port, killing a number of civilians but doing little material damage, and at once retraced his previous course in order to rendezvous with the *Breslau*. The British battle cruiser, *Indomitable,* with the *Indefatigable* not far behind, sighted the smoke of the German Dreadnought approaching her rapidly from the west just after 10.30 a.m.

A true calculation of the fighting power of the single German battle cruiser and the two British battle cruisers was very difficult to assess. On paper one of the British ships should have been almost a match for the *Goeben*. All the "I"-class battle cruisers carried a main armament of eight 12-inch guns, and could fire a broadside weight of shell of some 5,000 pounds. When the *Indomitable* had joined the fleet in 1908 she and her sisters were the wonder of their day, the first of a new generation of fighting ship, with an armament almost as great as a battleship's, and a speed much higher than that of the smaller armoured cruisers which they had made as obsolete as the *Dreadnought* had made all earlier battleships fit only for the breakers. Their inspiration had emanated from the fertile brain of Admiral Sir John Fisher, who believed in speed and hitting power and was prepared to sacrifice armour plate to obtain them. The German naval architects had quickly imitated them, but had given their ships much greater structural strength and weight of armour. Such was the speed of naval design development from 1908 that the latest German battle cruisers, including the *Goeben,* were quite as fast as the British ships, capable of withstanding much more punishment, and could still offer a roughly equal broadside weight from their 11-inch guns. The British naval authorities had a healthy respect for the power of the German battle cruisers.

Admiral Souchon had no illusions about the precariousness of his position when he caught sight of the *Indomitable* steaming towards him. In spite of the ever-growing power of their own fleet, and the high quality of their *matériel* and personnel, German naval officers continued to regard the Royal Navy with respect, and even with envy, for German naval tradition and history were negligible compared with Britain's, the Royal Navy was more numerous, and ship-for-ship the British vessels were larger, the calibre of the guns greater than the German's.

Souchon's respect for his future adversary was greater than it need have been. The war was to prove that even an earlier German battle cruiser was vastly superior to the "I"-class British equivalents—the *von der Tann* was to blow up the *Indefatigable* at Jutland in fifteen minutes. Souchon was as ignorant as Milne of the condition of the machinery of his opponent's ships. All the British battle cruisers were older than the *Goeben,* all were short of stokers; none had been in dock for some time, and the *Indomitable,* like the *Goeben,* was due for a refit.

The pursuit that followed the sighting off Bône on the morning of August 4th was in the nature of a challenge by both sides to show off their seamanship, and especially to conceal from the other their own inadequacies. The *Goeben* altered course to port and put on speed, the *Indomitable* altered to starboard to close. The *Goeben* turned away, and the two battle cruisers passed each other on opposite courses at a distance of five miles, guns trained warily fore and aft, but without saluting. The *Goeben* had already taken hostile action against Britain's allies, had already killed Frenchmen, but war between Britain and Germany had still not been declared, and the *Indomitable* had to content herself with swinging round in a wide circle behind the German vessel in an effort to keep her within range. Off Bizerta the

The fever of mutiny which spread through the Brazilian navy and which led to the shelling of Rio de Janeiro by the Minas Geraes *and her sister Dreadnought the* Sao Paulo *was inspired by the bloody seizure of the Portuguese warship* Dom Carlos *in the Tagus.*

"The mightiest broadside ever heard." The Brazilian battleship Minas Geraes is portrayed by a contemporary artist as her artillery thunders during gunnery trials. Impressive as this was, the

Combining vision, shrewdness, imagination, tact and an unbreakable pride, Sir Hugh Eustace Tennyson d'Eyncourt was the perfect salesman to confound Armstrong's competitors.

A romanticised boardroom portrait of Sir Andrew Noble, partner and successor to William Armstrong, and himself a benevolent gun-making despot.

On a rainy June day in 1914, "The Giant," now officially named Sultan Osman I eases down the River Tyne to Armstrong's Walker yard for her final fitting out. She was accompanied by the sounds of horns and sirens and the cheering of workers and spectators. Her masts were folded to allow clearance under bridges.

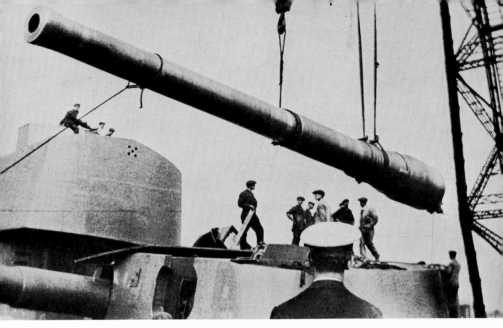

Now under the British Ensign and commissioned H. M. S. Agincourt, *the coveted and controversial warship receives the last of her 12-inch guns.* BELOW: *August, 1914. "The Gin Palace" with other Royal Navy Dreadnoughts on patrol. No other battleship could match her in number of guns, size or length. This photograph, taken looking aft, shows some of her 3-, 6- and 12-inch artillery.*

The man who was to command
her. Raouf Bey, Turkish hero
and brilliant naval commander,
aboard his cruiser, the Hamidieh.

The man who did command
her. Captain Douglas Romilly
Lothian Nicholson.

Cutting through a choppy sea, the Agincourt steams on patrol in 1915, her torpedo nets and "Marble Arch" flying boat decks removed

Mighty and dreadful, the Agincourt leads the Fourth Battle Squadron in a North Sea sweep in 1915. Less than a year later on May 31, 1916, the world's biggest battleship fulfilled the destiny for which she was built—full scale battle— in the great confrontation off the Danish Coast—the battle of Jutland.

Indomitable was joined by the *Indefatigable,* and in company with the light cruiser *Dublin* took up the chase in earnest. All through the heat of the day the stokers struggled to answer the call for more speed. Neither of the British battle cruisers could get within four knots of their best speed. For Souchon the issue was even more critical. Now that he knew his destination, and the hazards that lay between him and Constantinople, it was of crucial importance that he should not only escape from the British detachment before war was declared, but also "preserve *Goeben*'s reputation as the fastest ship in the Mediterranean", as the official German naval history described his situation, in order to dismay his pursuers, whose guns could not for long remain silent.

No Phoenician galley slaves ever strived more manfully in Mediterranean summer heat to escape an enemy than the stokers of the *Goeben*. Several of them fainted before the glare of the furnaces and had to be revived with buckets of water. Then, one after another, the old unreplaced tubes began to burst under the strain of the high pressure suddenly imposed upon them. Many stokers, stripped to the waist, were scalded and had to be treated for burns. One died at his post, two more were taken away unconscious and later succumbed. A fourth was burnt to death. They did not die in vain: the *Goeben*'s log showed she was still gaining speed and making almost 22 knots. In mid-afternoon a supreme effort was demanded of the exhausted men, sweltering and fainting in their inferno and fog of coal dust. Their courage was rewarded. By 4 o'clock it was clear that the British battle cruisers were falling behind. The *Goeben* was logging 24 knots. Half an hour later the tripod masts of the *Indomitable* and *Indefatigable* began to fade in the heat haze. The *Indefatigable* held on longer, then she too disappeared below the horizon, and only the little *Dublin,* a foe which could be blown out of the water at leisure, was left as shadower until dusk.

The *Indomitable* had been able to transmit the news that

the *Goeben* had been sighted, and Milne had passed on the news to the Admiralty in London, where the pursuit was followed with tense excitement. Unfortunately the direction of the pursuit had not been indicated, and Churchill presumed that, after their dawn bombardment, the Germans had continued westward in search of the French transports and to escape through the Straits of Gibraltar. All that the British battle cruisers had to do was to keep the *Goeben* within range, then open fire with the expiry of the British ultimatum to Germany at 11 p.m. British time. "Very good. Hold her. War imminent," signalled Churchill. But, thanks to a tenacious band of stokers, the quarry had already escaped.

On the first morning of war with Germany Admiral Milne was in a favourable position to take up the hunt again and destroy the enemy before sundown. He had every reason to believe that Admiral Souchon was back at Messina, and he had at his command the forces to bottle him up there until he was forced to emerge from one end or the other of the Straits of Messina that separated Sicily from the toe of Italy. Certainly the *Goeben* could not be long delayed in the Italian port for Italy had declared herself neutral. Nor did it seem likely to Milne that the German admiral would emerge from the southern exit of the straits, for to traverse their length would entail a serious infringement of Italian neutrality. Besides, his first instruction to prevent an attack on the French transports had never been cancelled, and his view—confirmed by the Admiralty—was that Souchon was still determined to break through to the west. It was in this direction that his main responsibilities lay, and he made his dispositions accordingly, the *Indomitable* being sent to coal at Bizerta, where she would be tactically well placed to join her two cohorts patrolling between Tunisia and Sicily. Light cruisers filled the gaps in the intercepting screen, only the *Gloucester* remaining on patrol off the southern exit of the Messina Straits to cover the unlikely event of a breakthrough to the east. Admiral Milne later

commented on his dispositions that his "first consideration
was the protection of the French transports from the German ships. I knew they had at least three knots greater
speed than our battle cruisers, and a position had to be
taken up from which the *Goeben* could be cut off if she
came westward."

To the west, with never a thought for the east! The inflexibility of the British admiral's mind was one of his chief
faults—Fisher had already called him, with characteristic
hyperbole, "an utterly useless commander". Certainly he
did not have the intellectual calibre to deal with as shrewd
a foe as Souchon, who also possessed all the usual advantages of the hunted—and some new friends in the east of
whom Milne knew nothing. And why should Milne have
known? He had no knowledge of the secret frenzied discussions taking place in Constantinople, nor that his country
had affronted Turkish pride and angered even the neutralist
element in the government by taking over its effective navy.
But Churchill knew how thick was the intrigue between
Enver Pasha and the German ambassador, and as the
Minister who had given the order to appropriate the Turkish
battleships he was in the best position to appreciate the possible consequences on relations with Turkey. But no one
at the Admiralty—and certainly not the First Lord—antici-
pated the German plan to snatch every diplomatic advantage from the new situation by offering the Turks the
Goeben and *Breslau* in compensation. Such blindness at first
appears hard to understand. Its cause can be found only in
Churchill's arrogant contempt for everything Turkish—
"scandalous, crumbling, decrepit, penniless Turkey"—itself only a reflection of Britain's imperial indifference to
the self-respect and well-being of the Ottoman Empire. In
British eyes it was curious that a foe as formidable as Germany should dabble in Islamic intrigues at all, and quite
inconceivable that these should seriously influence policy, to
the extent of sacrificing a powerful Dreadnought so sorely
needed in the German High Seas Fleet. No, the *Goeben* and

Breslau would try to break out to the west, and it was up to Milne to prevent such a disaster.

At Messina Souchon hoped rapidly to coal, and then, if the enemy permitted, to break through to the east before Milne had fully deployed his force. He had no illusions about his chances of success. Even if the French force were discounted—and the chances were that Lapeyrère would for the time being remain preoccupied with his troopships— Souchon was still faced with the task of evading three battle cruisers each of a power little less than his own, four armoured cruisers which, although old, together offered a considerable firepower, four modern light cruisers each quite as powerful as his own *Breslau,* a flotilla of destroyers and several submarines. Although he had shown his heels once to his pursuers, it was doubtful if he would again be able to do more than match the British battle cruisers' speed. Above all, he must not allow his vessel to be damaged. Even a single lucky shot fired at maximum range might do enough mechanical harm to reduce his speed by a few knots and bring him to bay. Souchon continued coaling as rapidly as possible, hustled on by the Italian port authorities who insisted that he must leave within 24 hours, and showed a further failure of hospitality by denying him normal wharfage facilities, which called for physical handling of every ton taken in. By mid-day on the 6th August Italian patience and the *Goeben*'s crew were alike exhausted and Souchon gave orders to hose down the ship, rest with a doubled beer ration, and depart at 5 p.m. His bunkers were little more than half full, and he would need to coal again in order to reach Constantinople. Furthermore, he had had disturbing news from Germany. There might, after all, be a little difficulty in gaining entry through the Dardanelles, as the Turks were still prevaricating, and it was thought inadvisable to try to make for Constantinople. Nor could the Austrians promise much in the way of help. The admiral was therefore left to make his own decision—a situation that quite matched his buccaneering inclinations, in spite of the ridiculous odds which faced him. Without more ado he decided, he wrote later, "to force the Turks, even against their will, to spread the war to the Black Sea against their ancient enemy, Russia".

It was still broad daylight when the German battle cruiser, followed twenty minutes later by her acolyte, steamed out of Messina and south through the straits, and then on to a north-easterly course as if for the Adriatic. The feint was of no avail. Captain Howard Kelly, the one British hero of the pursuit, picked up the ships at once from the *Gloucester,* signalled the enemy's position and course, and held on to his formidable quarry through the dusk and after darkness fell, guided by the smoke from the poor coal the Germans had collected at Messina, which showed up dense black against the star-lit sky. The *Gloucester* was still there at 10.45 p.m. when Souchon turned south-east for Cape Matapan. A minute later Kelly radioed this vital information to Milne, in spite of Souchon's efforts to jam his wireless.

The news came as no great surprise to Admiral Milne. The *Goeben* was not really going east, he reasoned. This was either a feint preparatory to fleeing north for Pola, or west for Gibraltar and the Atlantic. If the second was his destination, Milne could not be better placed to intercept him; so he remained where he was. If the *Goeben* was headed for the Adriatic, then it was up to Admiral Troubridge to intercept him with his four armoured cruisers.

Troubridge's naval roots went far back into the age of sail, and he was a popular and highly regarded commander. His appearance matched his reputation. He was burly without being overweight—a fine figure of a man—and tremendously handsome, carrying a thick mane of light blonde, almost white hair. His contempories speak of "his genial character" and "robust temperament". Troubridge at this time was following his instructions to watch the entrance to the Adriatic in case Austria came into the war against Britain. He was also expected to intercept and destroy the *Goeben* if she tried to break through to Pola, although he had earlier told his officers that he would engage the German ship only when circumstances—at dawn or in narrow waters— were favourable, believing that his squadron was no match for a single battle cruiser. Like Milne, Troubridge could not believe that the enemy was set on a south-easterly course and that Souchon would soon have to reveal his real intentions. He therefore turned north, hoping to catch Souchon at first light near Corfu. He knew that he was not supposed to attack "a superior force"—but what was meant by "superior"? His armoured cruisers each of 14,000 tons mounted in all twenty-two guns of 9.2-inch calibre, fourteen of 7.5-inch, and twenty of 6-inch against the *Goeben*'s ten 11-inch and twelve 5.9-inch. The total weight of his combined broadside was about a third again more than the *Goeben*'s, but having a higher rate of fire, he could theoretically throw a far greater weight of shell per minute than the German ship. He believed his force to have a maximum speed at least seven knots slower than the *Goeben*'s, having been as deceived as Milne by the German's freak burst of speed on that first day. Certainly the calculation of superiority between the two forces is difficult to define and has been hotly contested over the intervening years. But, in any case, Churchill was in fact referring to the Austrians when he used the loose term "a superior force".

Still holding on doggedly to the German battle cruiser, in bright moonlight and in constant danger of falling within range of the *Goeben*'s guns, Captain Kelly signalled again at midnight that the quarry was continuing to head south-east. On hearing this news Troubridge was at last persuaded to turn south, with the intention of intercepting the Germans before dawn and under conditions which would reduce the advantage of the enemy's heavier guns. But there was a counsel of even greater caution than his own in the flagship. At 2.45 a.m. Troubridge's Flag-Captain, Fawcet

Wray, who was a gunnery expert, asked him, "Are you going to fight, sir?" Troubridge told him that was his intention, even if it was against orders. Shortly after, Wray pressed his point again, and explained how the *Goeben* could circle round the four British ships and destroy them in turn. "It is likely to be suicide," Wray persisted. "I cannot turn away now, think of my pride," said the Admiral, whose great-grandfather had fought with Nelson at the Battle of the Nile. But Wray, a practical officer who knew all about guns, asked him to forget his pride: "It is your country's welfare which is at stake." When Troubridge's navigator confirmed that there was no possibility of closing the enemy's guns, Troubridge, now in tears, ordered the chase to be called off—"The bravest thing you have ever done in your life," commented the Flag-Captain. A few hours later, Troubridge was radioing his C-in-C that he had considered it "a great imprudence to place the squadron in such a position as to be picked off at leisure and sunk." And in spite of his advantage of four-to-one he stated that he "could never have got near her unless the *Goeben* wished to bring me to action".

In spite of this hasty retreat of the *Gloucester*'s sorely-needed reinforcements, Captain Kelly persisted in his single-handed pursuit all through the night, disregarding an order from Milne to drop astern so as to avoid capture. Souchon, unaware of the premature retreat of one enemy force and the distance that now separated him from the battle cruisers, then leisurely coaling at Malta, detached the *Breslau* in a final effort to throw off his shadow. The German cruiser first attempted to ride off the *Gloucester,* then when this failed tried bluff, holding off ahead and turning sharply to port and starboard as if dropping mines. Captain Kelly countered by opening fire at over 10,000 yards. The *Breslau* replied, and then the *Goeben,* fearing for her cohort, turned and opened up with her 11-inch guns. The *Gloucester* fell back from the great spouts of bursting 11-inch shells, and then when the *Goeben* resumed her eastward flight, turned

5 *

and followed once again. This was the hazardous art of shadowing practised at the highest level.

Back at Malta, Milne was becoming worried for his little cruiser. Her zeal might result in some injury, and besides she must be running short of coal, so he told Kelly not to go beyond Cape Matapan, and that he must then rejoin Admiral Troubridge. This time Captain Kelly obeyed his orders, with the result that at 4.40 p.m. on August 7th Admiral Souchon succeeded for the second time in throwing off the pursuit.

Little more than seven hours later, Admiral Milne was galvanized into action. He had all his three battle cruisers together again now at Malta, their bunkers full, their crews hot for action. At midnight he sailed out of Valetta harbour, and shaped course to the east, cruising very slowly. Some hours later he was signalled by the Admiralty, quite incorrectly, that the Austrians had entered the war. This dire news, reasoned Milne, clearly demanded the most serious new defensive dispositions for his fleet: they must not be caught divided, his scattered cruisers must be brought together again to fend off the new threat. A radio message went out to Troubridge to join him, the light cruisers were called in, all except two which were ordered to patrol in the Straits of Otranto to watch for signs of the new enemy. At mid-day the next day, August 9th, he was told that Britain was not after all at war with Austria, and that he was to go after the *Goeben* again. He did so at once, but as some of his cruisers had not yet arrived he limited his speed to 10 knots so that they could catch up before he engaged the enemy.

Meanwhile, Admiral Souchon, too, was experiencing troubles and anxieties. Having been shadowed so relentlessly to Cape Matapan, he expected to be picked up again among the Aegean Islands before he could take on more coal. And a head-on clash with half or even a third of the British force must end, he knew, only in annihilation. At Cape Maleas he was relieved to find one of his colliers faithfully awaiting him as ordered. But this was too public a place for the laborious and dangerous business of coaling, so he ordered her on to the lonely island of Denusa, where he joined her on the morning of August 9th. There he set up a look-out post on the highest point, and ordered coaling to begin, though steam was to be kept up in the boilers of his two ships so that they could leave within thirty minutes if a hostile masthead was sighted. Once again the German ratings, joined now by petty officers and officers, suffered the ordeal of manually coaling at sea in the intense Aegean summer heat. The sense of urgency and unknown danger were no less than they had been three days earlier, and Souchon himself remained as uncertain as ever of the position of his hunters and the reception he was likely to experience at his ultimate goal. Since his arrival in the Aegean he had received only one cryptic message by radio: the Turks, he was informed, were still making difficulties about his entry through the Dardanelles. Souchon dared not reply to this disturbing but ill-defined piece of information for fear of giving away his position, but it was essential that he should know more about conditions and circumstances before proceeding. He therefore despatched a second collier to Smyrna, where it was to act as a makeshift forward listening and receiving post with the German naval attaché in Constantinople. On arrival, the coaler's commander was ordered to radio: "Go to any lengths to arrange for me to pass through Straits at once with permission of Turkish Government if possible, without formal approval if necessary."

During all that day and for most of the night, the German Admiral awaited a reply in a state of acute anxiety. It was remarkable that he had not heard any more of the British, and he found the enemy's apparent strict radio silence unnerving. They must now, he knew, at least be proceeding towards the Aegean Islands, if they were not already in close proximity. And this time, at last, Souchon's belief was justified. Still steaming at a leisurely half speed, Admiral

Milne with his powerful force passed the Cervi Channel and entered the Aegean in search of his quarry at 3 a.m. on the morning of August 10th.

At almost precisely this moment, the *Goeben*'s wireless room picked up the first re-transmitted message from Smyrna. "Enter," ran the terse signal. "Demand surrender of forts. Capture pilot." Before daylight, the *Goeben* and *Breslau* were on their way, fully coaled for the last lap, their crews ready for action and buoyed up with new confidence now that uncertainty was over, that their destination, or at least a clash of arms, was near at hand. The two ships threaded their way through the Aegean Islands, between Chios and Psara, past Lesbos and Baba Cape. By late afternoon on August 10th the Plains of Troy were in sight, and at five o'clock they anchored off the heavily fortified entrance to Cape Helles. A signal requesting a pilot was hoisted. A boat put out. Its answering signal was one of the most fateful of the war: "Follow me."

Enver Pasha and his followers, supported by the persuasion of Baron von Wangenheim, General von Sanders, Colonel von Kress and all the intimidating might of the German Military Mission, had won the crucial contest in Constantinople; and the sight of the little destroyer putting out from Constantinople to meet and escort in the German Dreadnought and its accompanying cruiser appeared to summarize the triumph of the German cause in the drawn-out battle of wits and threats which had lasted a full week in the Turkish capital. The Turkish navy had its Dreadnoughts, after all, and that was something to be thankful for, even if the circumstances of its arrival were not according to expectation.

For where were Captain Raouf Bey and his gallant crew? No matter. This great vessel was a present, a gift from the German Emperor. And Admiral Souchon later ordered his men to don fezzes to complete the impression. Moreover, the nameplate "Goeben" was replaced by a new one, "Sultan Selim". This sounded almost as magnificent as

"Sultan Osman", and the German battlecruiser was certainly a formidable looking vessel—one which had outwitted the British.

At one time Admiral Milne had been little more than a hundred miles behind his quarry, and he had listened anxiously to the sound of radio messages between the German colliers. For more than twelve hours after his adversary had passed the Chanak fortresses and entered the Sea of Marmora, he remained under the impression that he was closing in on the enemy. Still confident that Souchon's destination must be either Pola or the Atlantic—although he was anxious that Port Said or Alexandria might be bombarded on the way—Milne despatched scouting cruisers among the islands, and patrolled his battle cruisers to cut off the German line of retreat. His surprise was great indeed when at mid-day on August 11th he received a radio message informing him that the *Goeben* was at Constantinople. "So that unhappy affair ended," wrote Corbett, "in something like a burst of public derision that the Germans should so soon have been chased out of the Mediterranean to suffer an ignominious internment. How false was that consolation none but the best informed could then even dream. It was many months before it was possible to appreciate fully the combined effrontery, promptitude and sagacity of the move. When we consider that the Dardanelles was mined, that no permission to enter it had been ratified, and that everything depended on the German powers of cajolery at Constantinople, when we also recall the world-wide results that ensued, it is not too much to say that few naval decisions more bold and well-judged were ever taken."*

The consequences of the escape of the German force were unhappy for Admiral Milne and several of his subordinates. For a time the impression was sustained that Souchon had

* *History of the Great War: Naval Operations*, Vol. I by Sir Julian S. Corbett (1920).

been driven into his funk-hole by British naval might. The Admiralty's official press announcement approved entirely of the C-in-C's conduct. Then when Turkey came into the war on the German side, and Fisher replaced Battenberg as First Sea Lord, the matter was reconsidered, the questions and accusations began to fly. Milne was informed by Churchill that he would not be succeeding to his next command, and was informally dubbed "Sir Berkeley Goeben" by a furious Fisher. He took no further active part in the war. Troubridge was subjected to a Court of Inquiry, and then a Court Martial, which acquitted him of the main charge of forbearing "to pursue the chase of His Imperial German Majesty's ship *Goeben,* being an enemy then flying . . ." But like his C-in-C he never again served afloat. And, as a result of the evidence tendered at the Court Martial, Captain Wray's service career, as well as his social position, were shattered.

As to the ships, their fate was no less melancholy. All but two of Milne's largest ships were lost at Jutland, these casualties representing no less than five-sixths of the total British loss of armoured ships in that battle. There were few survivors.

The British government responded sharply to the news of the arrival of the *Goeben* and *Breslau* at Constantinople, and to the Turkish government's refusal to evict the German crews and demilitarize the vessels. Privately, neither Winston Churchill nor the Foreign Secretary, Sir Edward Grey, had any illusions about the situation. "This means that Turkey has joined Germany and may attack Egypt," said Grey. Publicly, British communications to Turkey continued their upbraiding, hectoring, condescending tone. Churchill suggested that the Royal Navy should send destroyers up the Bosporus to torpedo the German ships; but Lord Kitchener, the Secretary of State for War, would have none of this. Grey protested about the continued presence of the

German ships, and was told by the Turkish government that they had been bought to offset new Greek naval power. To demonstrate the innocence of their intentions, the Turkish government proposed that they should be put under the control of the British Naval Mission and Admiral Limpus, who remained in Constantinople as an uneasy and helpless spectator, longing to return to active service with the Grand Fleet. The British Prime Minister, Herbert Asquith, wrote privately that Britain would be insisting on the replacement of the German crews by Turks; and a further protest to Constantinople followed. Winston Churchill wrote of his seizure of the Turkish battleships in Britain, and the crisis in Constantinople that followed this step and the escape of Admiral Souchon: "The Sequestration (of the *Sultan Osman* and *Rashadieh*) angered not only the Turkish government but large numbers of patriotic Turks throughout the country. Moreover, in the struggles which ensued in Constantinople and in the Turkish Cabinet between the Turkish war party and those who favoured neutrality, this episode seemed to have weight. I did my best, with the approval of the Cabinet, to allay the legitimate heartburnings of the Turkish Ministry of Marine."* The impact of the seizure on the common people, and the way in which it helped the German cause, could be better appreciated by Englishmen still in Constantinople. "It is not too much to say," wrote one, "that it was the most powerful weapon which the German party possessed in Constantinople against the British government ... The papers inspired by Germany spoke of the act as piracy, as a blow aimed solely at Turkey. It was a bully's attack on a small state"†

Two days after Souchon's arrival at Constantinople—where he had been cheered in the streets as if he were Raouf Bey himself, and had been wined and dined by the War Party—Churchill sent to Sir Edward Grey his recommendations on the next British moves to counteract the German

* *The World Crisis,* Vol. I.
† *Forty Years in Constantinople.*

coup. "The British Embassy," he wrote, "assisted if necessary by the English Naval Mission, should assure that all the
Germans leave at once, and that the ships are definitely
handed over to the Turkish navy. In these circumstances
the Admiralty would allow the Naval Mission to remain,
as requested by the Grand Vizier. The Turks could also
be informed, that after the war is over, we should be quite
ready in principle, as far as we can now foresee, to transfer
one or both of the two ships we have requisitioned to their
flag, and that we are quite ready to negotiate with them
at the present time in regard to payment of the sums due to
Turkey."

The subtle art of procrastination was to be practised by
Turkey for several more weeks yet, but already the days had
gone when she could be treated with the old arrogant dis-
dain. Already Talaat Bey and his cronies had acquired control of the country's organs of communication and propaganda. On August 16th Admiral Limpus and his staff were
told that their services were no longer required, and German
officers appeared mysteriously on board other Turkish warships and among the guns guarding the Dardanelles and the
Bosporus. Suddenly, there were Germans everywhere. And
yet "the party which stood for neutrality contained men
who, lacking though they were in any material means of
enforcing their views, could not easily be ignored";* and
in mid-October, with German patience utterly exhausted,
Turkey was still hanging on to neutrality, by the slenderest
of threads. Admiral Souchon finally cut this on October 28th
by sailing from Constantinople under Turkish colours, and
in company with several Turkish men-of-war on the following morning, shelling Odessa and other Russian ports. Faced
with this *fait accompli,* and the 11-inch guns of the *Sultan
Selim* (late *Goeben*) now back in port, the Turkish neutral-
ists surrendered. By November 5th Britain, France as well
as Russia were at war with Turkey.

Thus the stain of combat spread and there soon began

* Mallet's despatch.

one of the bloodiest campaigns of the whole First War. The Dardanelles were closed, all lines to Russia through the Black Sea were severed, Egypt, the oilfields of the Middle East, Imperial India itself, were placed in jeopardy. Diplomatic incompetence, blind unimaginativeness, and at sea confusion of control and signalling combined with irresolution had all played their part in this tragedy of errors. But all this only made up the train of events between two batteries of naval guns: the massive 12-inch broadside of the *Sultan Osman* in the River Tyne in England, denied to the Turkish navy by the British; and the 11-inch broadside of the *Sultan Selim** in the Bosporus, a present from the Kaiser, silently intimidating the Grand Vizier and the Sultan.

* These two Dreadnoughts established a number of historical records. Not only was the *Sultan Osman I* the longest, heaviest and most heavily gunned battleship of her day; but the *Sultan Selim,* later renamed *Yavuz* served through two wars, was the first capital ship to be bombed from the air, and had the longest active life of any Dreadnought: from 1912 until only a few years ago.

CHAPTER SEVEN

The Battle

The big battleship, whose seizure by Winston Churchill had caused such heartburning and such loss to her owners, was accepted by the Royal Navy with a sorry show of reluctance. This monster was, after all, something of a compulsory adoptee, possessing as it did many unfamiliar features which are the mark of a child of another's loins. No officer of the Admiralty's design department would have specified such an exaggerated length, such a multitude of guns, such disregard for structural strength, such lightly protected magazines for her vast store of shells and their propellent. It was not unusual for British shipbuilders to use as guinea-pigs the warships built for foreign navies for the purpose of testing out certain radical equipment and aspects of design which a more conservative and cautious British Admiralty was likely to reject. This Dreadnought was heavily endowed with prototype equipment, and certain responsible officers in the Admiralty were not happy about it. In the eyes of many people, her very size told against her. If the Royal Navy had considered a main armament of fourteen heavy guns desirable for a battleship, they would have built several such vessels by now. Fourteen heavy guns? Twenty 6-inch guns? A full load displacement of over 30,000 tons? These statistics were slightly ridiculous, and certainly ostentatious to the point of vulgarity. She was, in short, a suspect giant.

Then there was something else: she had a stain on her

reputation. She had been in the hands of her builders for a suspiciously long time. Battleships for the Royal Navy (they might be smaller and might boast fewer guns) which had been laid down after her had been commissioned months earlier. And she had, after all, been rejected by her first owners. Even those unpredictable South Americans had not wanted her. They had said they could not afford her—or was that the real reason? What about the rumour that she could never fire a full broadside with full charges from all those guns, not without the recoil breaking her back?

However, the big battleship was theirs, thanks to the foresight and quick action of the First Lord, and the Grand Fleet was in no condition to refuse Dreadnoughts. Admiral Jellicoe's margin of strength over Admiral Friedrich von Ingenohl's High Seas Fleet being further narrowed by the absence in the Mediterranean of a number of his battle cruisers, which were at that time reported to be chasing out of that sea a couple of German warships. So a commander was appointed and told to re-equip and modify his ship in any way that he thought necessary (so long as it did not take more than a few weeks); and she was, for the second time in the year, renamed. They could hardly have chosen a more ringing name than *Agincourt*. The Grand Fleet, always ready with a waggish colloquialism, at once retitled her "The Gin Palace". On St. Crispin's Day, too, the gin flowed freely in her wardroom; and the rum flowed freely in the seamen's flats, where the ship's chant rang out:

> "Then happy and chatty and happy are we
> Upon the old Agin-c-o-u-r-t.
>
> We don't give a damn if it rains or it snows
> As long as we go where the old Agy goes."

To find at short notice a battleship's company of some eleven hundred officers and men presented the Admiralty with a problem. Most of the reserves had been mobilized in June for the July Royal Fleet Review, shrewdly laid on by Churchill in anticipation of war with Germany. To man the *Agincourt* the Admiralty was reduced to drawing from the highest and lowest echelons of the service: the Royal yachts, and the detention barracks. The Royal yachts, by tradition, were manned by picked ratings and privileged officers with special qualities or special connections in Royal circles.

At the beginning of August, the *Victoria and Albert* was still in Portsmouth harbour, where she had been used by King George V for his Royal Review—the fleet had taken six hours, at 15 knots, to pass his yacht. Her Commodore was Douglas Romilly Lothian Nicholson, and he was at once appointed the *Agincourt's* captain: a worthy replacement for Captain Raouf Bey, who, with his fellow officers and the entire complement of the *Neshid Pasha* had disappeared from Tyneside without trace a few hours after the seizure. Captain Nicholson, like Raouf Bey, was an officer with an aggressive bent and an unusual skill at seamanship, but quite lacked the Turk's devious political mind. "He was," said one of his officers, "a delightful man and a great gentleman." He had been nicknamed "White Nick" for his fair hair and fresh complexion, and in a service with many namesakes, to distinguish him from "Thumby Nick", who lacked a thumb; and from "Black Nick", of a dark and threatening demeanour, another senior naval officer. Nicholson brought his commander with him, one Denis Grenville-Thynne, a short-tempered officer with a hook nose who loved destroyers and despised big ships as effete. The engineer commander was Reginald W. Skelton, who had been on Scott's expedition to the South Pole. Responsibility for the *Agincourt's* numerous guns rested with Commander Valentine Gibbs, a great athlete and bobsleigh and skeleton champion, who contrived to defeat year after year every American effort to wrest the title from him on the Cresta Run; and now demonstrated his speed in securing from Armstrongs the last elusive big gun and having it mounted. His assistant was none other than Lieutenant Frank Elliott. After doing his best to introduce some basic knowledge of gunnery into the raw Turkish recruits, this officer had been despatched by Admiral Limpus from Constantinople to meet his charges on board the *Sultan Osman* at Tyneside, proceed on the battleship's gunnery trials with them, and continue their education on the voyage back to Turkey. He now found himself recalled to his own service and demoted to his old rank of lieutenant, but with more experienced gun crews in his charge.

These officers of the *Agincourt* made an oddly-assorted company. Few of them had ever served in a battleship before. Some had never been to sea in an armed vessel, among them Surgeon-Captain C. G. Bankhart, and his reservist assistant, Lieutenant A. F. R. Woolaston, a notable explorer among the pygmies of Borneo, who survived the war only to be shot dead by a mad undergraduate when he became a don at King's College, Cambridge. Then there was the ship's chaplain, Hugh Embling, an earnest young Anglican priest of strong character, who considered all the officers past redemption, and later became the Bishop of Korea; and Angus Cunninghame Graham, son of one of King George V's grooms-in-waiting, Commander C. E. F. Cunninghame Graham, M.V.O., R.N.

On August 3rd, 1914, the ship's company of the *Victoria and Albert* knew nothing of the seizure of the *Sultan Osman* up at Newcastle. Indeed, few of them knew anything at all of the ship; only that, months earlier, they had heard that the biggest battleship in the world had been sold by Brazil to Turkey, an event of only minor interest to them. The dominant topic of conversation was the war which had already broken out in Europe, and the certainty of imminent British participation. They all knew that their days of splendour and luxury in the Royal Yacht were numbered, and all looked forward with relish to active service in a fighting ship. A posting signal was hourly expected.

Late in the afternoon of August 3rd this signal arrived,

ordering most of the officers, warrant officers and men to proceed that evening to Tyneside in order to commission a new battleship. No one present knew of a British battleship completing on the Tyne, and no one had heard of the *Agincourt*. There was much speculation about the identity of the vessel, which was not listed in Jane or Brassey; and it was some time before one of the officers suggested that their signal must refer to the Turkish super-Dreadnought *Sultan Osman I*. On the long, hot, wakeful train journey to the north that night the big battleship was discussed at length amongst the officers in their first-class compartments, as well as among the ratings. "She is," wrote one officer proudly in his diary, "the largest warship afloat."

In the early hours of the last day of peace for Britain, this advance party from the Royal Yacht made their way from the Central Station at Newcastle downstream to Armstrong's new Walker yard. "She was a tremendous sight, none of us had ever seen anything like her before," one lieutenant commented on the moment when he first sighted the *Agincourt*. On that brilliantly sunny August morning when the first of her company came aboard for the first time, relieving from their guard duty the detachment of Sherwood Foresters, they saw her in the full perfection of her grace and beauty—as Tennyson d'Eyncourt had drawn her for the Brazilian Minister of Marine more than three years earlier.

Their sense of wonder was renewed when they came aboard. Everywhere they looked there were the barrels of guns—3-inch guns behind shields or in ports, 6-inch guns in a long battery in the upper deck, behind shields on the forecastle deck, and higher yet in the bridges fore and aft; 12-inch guns in turrets, seven of them, one for every day in the week, as someone observed, and from that time the turrets were named—forward to aft—from Sunday to Saturday. Below decks, everyone was overwhelmed by the impression of size and spaciousness, although there were misgivings among some of the officers, and one remarked, "She's no ship to be torpedoed in!"

No rating had ever before seen a mess deck like this. Compared with the business-like seamen's flats in a British warship, the *Agincourt*'s was like a dance hall, with room for games between the mess tables, and a wide choice of places to sling hammocks. There were even—and this caused some exclamations of disbelief—fixed bunks for some of the ratings. On the discovery of the Islamic latrines, expletives of a different nature—a blend of righteous indignation and mirth—echoed from the steel decks and bulkheads. No one had seen anything like *these* before either. The officers were equally impressed by their own living quarters, by their individual cabins ("Like the ruddy *Mauretania*!" as one of them remarked, with opening ports: armour plate normally prohibited such a luxury on British Dreadnoughts) and their wardroom, which was larger by far than any they had ever seen, with its cretonne-covered or leather armchairs and sofas arranged neatly about low mahogany coffee tables, its fine Turkish rugs on the polished teak decking, silk-shaded lights and beautifully panelled-over bulkheads. Those officers who had previously commissioned a new vessel straight from the builders were surprised by the cleanliness and ship-shape order of things. Usually it took several weeks to clear the builders left-over rubbish and clean down the ship. But judging by the spotless condition of the *Agincourt,* it was clear that Armstrongs had made strenuous efforts to meet the demands of Raouf Bey. Even the cutlery and crockery and linen—all of the highest quality and inscribed in Turkish—were ready for immediate use; as were the highly polished brass spitoons which had been provided for the convenience of the strict Moslems among the Turkish officers who preferred not to swallow their saliva during times of fast.

But this fine vessel, so richly equipped with the comforts and conveniences of a luxury liner, was now a fighting ship of the Royal Navy, as Captain Nicholson soon made clear to his officers and ratings. The country was at war, the ship was badly needed up at Scapa Flow, and must be made ready for action. The exclamations and the ribald jokes at the new discoveries might continue for a while yet, but no sooner had the men stowed their kit than they were set to work. The following days were full of activity. Drafts of men arrived daily from naval depots all over the country, and from the detention camps where all but the hardened cases had had their sentences remitted. Assisted by Armstrong's workmen, the hands worked day and night getting in stores and provisions. Now that the ship's ammunition could be taken on board, the shells had to be fused. Hundreds of tallies had to be unscrewed and reversed, to reveal their legend in English, while others—a remnant from a more distant past and still bearing their message in Portuguese—had to be replaced. Day by day the ship began to assume a more familiar, a more British guise. The same plumbers who six months earlier had replaced the Brazilian latrine fittings with the exotic yet somehow indecent "squatters", were now employed, on overtime and through the night, in wrenching them out again, sealing off the cold taps and securing paper-holders, and re-equipping them with proper Western sanitary equipment, varying from the highest quality decorated water closets for Captain Nicholson, down to the standard service issue for the ratings.

Captain Nicholson, unlike a number of ship's commanders who stripped their vessels in a fervour of warlike spirit of almost every luxurious or inflammable fitting, did not insist on converting the *Agincourt* overnight into an austere steel shell. Not even the wardroom suffered seriously, being deprived of only its rugs and curtaining and some of the coffee tables; although the wardroom annexe, which had been provided for the uncouth Turkish engineer officers, was appropriated by the ship's chaplain and converted into a chapel. The officers' quarters remained more spacious and elegant than those of any other battleship in the Grand Fleet. However, the *Agincourt*'s fighting efficiency was taken seriously by her new captain, who had decided as a first measure that her famous "Marble Arch" spanning her midships turrets must be removed to allow greater freedom for four of her big guns and, because of the inflammable nature of the boats and hammocks stowed inside and on them, to reduce the fire risk. On August 9th a great floating crane came alongside and removed the two sections in turn. The balance of her rig was instantly destroyed, but the greater exposure of these two turrets added further to her aggressive appearance and the loss of her top hamper made her appear even longer and rangier.

On August 20th the *Agincourt* was completed with three hundred tons of coal, and two days later she was at last ready for sea, and for her war service, though she was still an untried vessel and manned by as mixed a company as any in the Royal Navy. Only a scattering of the citizens of Newcastle, to whom the vessel had for so long been a source of pride and wonder and employment, saw her leave. For her departure was also an event of great importance to the German navy, and to Admiral Tirpitz who had heard with anxiety of her seizure by the enemy: only the more recent German Dreadnoughts carried an armament of 12-inch guns, and none could fire a broadside of more than ten heavy guns, compared with the fourteen of the *Agincourt*. Shortly before her expected day of sailing, a German mine-layer had crept in to the East coast and laid her mines thirty miles off the mouth of the Tyne, and several suspected German spies, pursued by mocking children, had already been arrested in Newcastle by guards who had been posted strategically around the Walker shipyard and on the City's bridges.

The *Agincourt* slipped her moorings in the early hours of August 25th and proceeded in darkness stern first down the Tyne at 4.30 a.m. towed by five tugs, which she cast off in the estuary. Now under her own power, she passed unharmed through the German minefield, of which her lookouts saw nothing, and when well out of sight of land she dropped her pilot and the Armstrong officials who had remained on board to ensure that all was well. In bright mid-morning sunshine and a flat calm, the ship was swung to adjust her compasses, then Captain Nicholson ordered the decks cleared for his ship's first gun trials.

For any warship, the first firing of her guns is an occasion of special significance. A battleship is no more than a platform for its guns. The hull has been constructed to support them, the engines to propel them towards their target, the armour plate to protect them and their ammunition, their elaborate sighting equipment to ensure their accuracy. The firing of her batteries is the culmination of all the expensive years of planning and endeavour that have been devoted to the man-of-war, from the distant time when her designer makes the first mark on his drawing board, through all the forging and casting, the bending and riveting, to her launching and final completion. For the *Agincourt,* the ignition of her first cordite propellent, the recoil that shook her every plate from stem to stern, the sight of that white muzzle flash with its scarlet heart, all made an indelible mark on the minds of every member of the ship's company who witnessed it. For many this was the first experience of heavy gun-firing, and few had experienced the compound of fear and sense of power which the convulsive shock of a firing 12-inch naval gun offers to those in close proximity to it. A further degree of drama was added to this occasion by the consciousness of imminent peril. For three weeks through sultry summer heat, amid reports of critical combats in France and Belgium, the men of the *Agincourt* had been striving to get their Dreadnought ready for sea, spurred on by the knowledge that theirs was the mightiest in the world and was desperately needed by the commander-in-chief, that battle with the Germans— towards which their lives for so long had been prepared— might occur at any moment: "the mighty clash of arms in the North Sea" of which so much had been written over fifteen years of tense rivalry.

The gun trials of the *Agincourt* were especially memorable for another reason. Nothing could deprive them of their significance, but they included an element of disappointment—even of anti-climax—for her gun crews and gunnery officers and petty officers, and for the Royal Marines who were responsible for two of the ship's turrets. For it had to be admitted that the guns did not work very well; that there was, after all, some justification for the doubts of some of the Admiralty officials about the fighting efficiency of this vast and eccentric vessel. For reasons of safety it had been decided that a full broadside of all fourteen guns should not yet be attempted, nor that full charges should be used. But not one of the guns would fire at all when the first attempts were made using the normal electrical method, and it was not until the more primitive emergency percussion firing method was resorted to that anything happened. Then the new-fangled experimental "churn lever" gave a lot of trouble. This piece of equipment was intended to speed up and simplify the reloading and firing of the heavy guns, and was operated by one man, rather like the gear shift of a motor car. A single master lever was pivoted at its foot in the centre of a steel case. At the top end it had four steel hooks which engaged one at a time in the sides of the box and at the same time with four separate levers mounted on the sides of the box. By manipulating this lever, in turn the gun was hydraulically brought down to a fixed loading position, its breech was opened, the ammunition cage was raised, and the charge was rammed home. This gadget had unfortunately not been perfected by Armstrongs before being installed in the *Agincourt*. It was also at first suspected of being responsible for a further and more serious failing in the battleship's ordnance. For it was discovered during these first trials that many of the shells simply broke up in flight. This did not actually occur as they left the gun's muzzle, and so did not endanger the structure of the ship itself. But there was no denying that, at least for the present, the big battleship was less of a threat to any enemy, and also more of a threat to any friendly ship that happened to be passing beneath the flight of her shells, and especially to escorting destroyers.

A number of theories were put forward as a cause for this somewhat fundamental failing. At first it appeared that the shells themselves might be at fault, especially when it was discovered that some of them appeared to have been drawn from the bottom of the navy's reserve supplies, carrying the stencil mark "Repaired 1892". The guns, too, were suspected. The butt strap, which was shrunk on to link the "A" and "B" tubes of the 45-feet-long barrel, was thought fractionally to impede and so weaken the shell in its passage that it fell to pieces in mid-air. But the most widely accepted cause was that the cone at the front end of the loading chamber of the gun, where the rifling began, was of faulty design, so that when the shell was driven hard forward the serrated copper driving band shrunk on to its end did not engage firmly into the barrel, causing the shell to assume an aslant position and to suffer an intolerable lateral strain when the charge was fired. This was by no means an invariable occurrence, and the ratio of failures tended to fall off as the gun warmed to its task. Nevertheless, it was a disquieting experience, and the failing was never completely cured during the life of the ship. It also added one more eccentric legend to add to her "squatters", her Eastern exotic luxuries, Brazilo-Turkish heredity, her immoderate statistics, that singled out the ship from its cohorts in the Grand Fleet; and any reference to "The Gin Palace" or "the old Agy", usually led to some quip.

If the gunfiring trials of the *Agincourt* were a technical disappointment, the thunder of her guns—the harmless break-up of the shells notwithstanding—added evidence of reality to the warlike spirit of her ship's company; and they were sustained by a new spirit of vigour and purpose as their Dreadnought sped north towards Scapa Flow at her best cruising speed of 18 knots. At 5.30 the following morning, the *Agincourt* sighted part of the British Battle Fleet, and followed the ships into Scapa Flow.

Scapa Flow was the Grand Fleet's main base, a bleak, inhospitable anchorage in the Orkney Islands, beyond the most northerly point of the Scottish mainland. The featureless islands that protected this anchorage enjoyed names like Fara, Hoy, Burray and Flotta, and the headlands were called Sneuk, Grim or Hoxa in case there should be any doubt of the legendary Celtic origins of the place. Here, for the next four years, the greater part of the Grand Fleet spent the greater part of its time; according to the extremes of prejudice either threatening to dry-dock itself on its own empty cans, or sustaining from afar British maritime control and the blockade of Germany. At Scapa the dominant colour was nearly always grey, the grey ships on the grey sea against the grey sky and the background of the bleak grey islands. When it was not raining often a fine mist fell from the eternal grey clouds, reducing still further the visibility. It was grey and misty when the *Agincourt* anchored for the first time on the morning of August 26th.

Sombre the scene may have been, but it was also immensely impressive and comforting, for here was assembled the full might of British naval power, the greatest force the world had ever seen: line after line of battleships and cruisers and destroyers, with countless attendant colliers and oil tankers, supply ships, store ships, hospital ships and frozen meat ships—a vast concourse of vessels of all kinds, and all dedicated to the single purpose of keeping secure and mobile the heavy guns of the Dreadnoughts. Among them, then, on this grey misty August morning there came the biggest of them all, to become at once a source of speculation and wonder. There was no other vessel there remotely resembling the *Agincourt*—no other with more than five centre-line turrets, against the *Agincourt*'s seven, no other with a length exceeding six hundred feet. The legends and anecdotes of her past, the curiously mixed nature of her complement, all these had still to be learned. But almost from the time of her anchoring, by reason of her distinctive size and silhouette, she became an identification mark in the Grand Fleet. Objects were distinguished in relation to the big battleship, and at sea it became a common and convenient practice to give orders to ships to take station so many points to port or starboard of the *Agincourt*.

The new reinforcement at once became the object of interested attention. Friends of her officers came across the water by boat to roam her wardroom and cabin flats, and there were many exclamations at her size and the luxury of her accommodation. No ship in the navy, it was generally agreed, could be more comfortable to serve in in times of peace, but in battle—well, they would sooner be well clear of those vast and lightly protected magazines, and no one was prepared to give her much of a chance if a torpedo found its mark.

On the following day the Commander-in-Chief was piped aboard to inspect more formally his new vessel, and both Winston Churchill and Jellicoe made a further admiring examination of the vessel shortly afterwards.

Only three days after the *Agincourt* left Newcastle on her first commission, the Battle of Heligoland Bight was fought. This was a confused cruiser action, in which the Germans lost four ships and some one thousand men. The expectations of a general action between the main fleets remained high in the Grand Fleet, and everything seemed to point to a glorious war career for the *Agincourt*. No one was better endowed to bring this about than Captain Nicholson. Although he had been brought up in sail, had been through the debilitating spit-'n-polish era in the Royal Navy, had reached senior rank when un-Nelsonian caution and defensiveness governed the spirit and strategy of the service, and had held the un-warlike command of the Royal Yacht up to the outbreak of war, "White Nick" had made a close study of war at sea and showed himself worthy of his ship's name and her numerous guns. He fretted at Jellicoe's policy of caution and at the inflexibility of the Grand Fleet Battle Instructions, and acquired for his ship a reputation for unorthodox aggressiveness. But the pugnacious spirit of Captain Nicholson—and of so many other officers and ratings in the Grand Fleet—was to be frustrated for many months yet. The policy of the German naval command was no less timid than that of the British, and after two minor defeats in the North Sea within the first months of the war the German commander became even more reluctant to expose his main battle fleet to the superior gunpower of the Royal Navy.

Except for practice shoots, then, the guns of the *Agincourt* remained silent. Much of the old Victorian ammunition was replaced, and every measure was tried to prevent the unfortunate breaking-up of her shells in flight. The accuracy of her gunnery greatly improved under "Val" Gibbs, whose demands sometimes seemed relentless to the gun crews. Whenever the opportunity occurred he would obtain the services of a tug or steam drifter to tow a target, and a shoot was carried out in the anchorage of Scapa Flow itself with sub-calibre guns, two-pounder guns being screwed into the breeches of the 12-inch, and rifles attached to the 6-inch. This offered in miniature a replica of a full shoot, so that range-takers, gunlayers, trainers and sight-setters, and the spotting officers all had good practice, although only the ammunition loading numbers had an easy time. Month by month Gibbs brought the *Agincourt's* gunnery to an ever higher state of efficiency, so that it became less easy to mock the big battleship for its ostentatious display of gun barrels and more difficult to deny her claim to have the sharpest gun crews in the Grand Fleet. From time to time full calibre shoots in the Pentland Firth, the strip of water between Scotland and the Orkneys, were ordered, and the ship would go out escorted by two destroyers (the fear of submarines was ever present) and a tug to tow the battle practice target. Reduced charges of

two or three instead of four silk bags of cordite propellant
were still normally used on these shoots to save gun barrel
wear, and rarely were more than four guns fired together as
a salvo. Greater confidence was slowly built up in the big
ship's ordnance by these shoots, and gradually the old belief
that she would break her back if a full broadside of fourteen
guns was fired with full charges began to diminish among
the gunnery officers. The men, however, retained a lingering
anxiety on this vexed speculation, and elsewhere in the Grand
Fleet it was widely accepted as a matter of course and as
something of a joke that "The Gin Palace" would break her
back—if she did not blow up first—when she fired her first
full broadside. It stood to reason, if not to science, some
people said: you only had to run your eye over her length,
then count her guns.

One afternoon, when she was alone at gun firing practice
north of Ireland, it was determined to put the matter to the
test once and for all. The result was shattering and memorable, and justified every fine calculation made by Tennyson d'Eyncourt, Perrett, and the design team of Armstrongs.
There was not a stoved-in bulkhead, not a twisted plate or
rib in the vessel. But it was a nerve-shattering business that
was not to be repeated until the need arose. The broadside
of ten big guns in a British battleship was a thunderous business not often indulged in. Many of the *Agincourt*'s company had never suffered even this impact. With almost half
as many guns again the concussion was well-nigh unbearable. No one escaped it, even down in the engine room. The
Turkish crockery and glass were smashed in hundreds, and
the coal dust found its way out of the bunkers and per-
colated everywhere. For days afterwards the men were still
picking it out of their bunks and hammocks and their
clothes. Once was enough. But of course none of the other
ships believed the story, and the *Agincourt* retained her
reputation that she was the only ship the Germans could
never sink because she would do it herself first.

The likelihood of "The Gin Palace" meeting the enemy and again risking the recoil strain of her guns firing in anger seemed to diminish as the months passed. At first the Grand Fleet was often at sea. Scapa Flow, it was soon discovered, was almost entirely undefended as a base, especially against the depredations of the submarine. Its vulnerability as an anchorage was never proven as dramatically as was Pearl Harbor's twenty-seven years later, but the absence of proper protection to the massive fleet on which Britain wholly depended as a maritime power was there for all to see. The range and power of the German U-boat had been grossly underestimated—by the Germans as much as by the British. After three British armoured cruisers were sunk in turn within an hour on September 22nd, 1914, by a single submarine off the Dutch coast, with a loss of nearly 1500 lives, a submarine fever—"periscopitis"—seized the British fleet. In a choppy sea it was easy to imagine a periscope, and there were frequent claimed sightings—nearly all false—and much excited firing of guns at porpoises, floating wreckage, and even at waves. It was decided that the Grand Fleet was safer at sea, on the move, surrounded by destroyer screens. After the supposed sighting of a periscope within Scapa Flow itself, Admiral Jellicoe pulled out his entire armada and withdrew to his Irish bases. It was not until late in November 1914 that Scapa Flow was considered secure enough for the Grand Fleet to return.

Of her first eighty days with the Grand Fleet the *Agincourt* had spent forty at sea, proving herself an admirable sea boat in all weathers. But there now lay ahead a year and a half of inaction that was to be broken only by occasional North Sea "sweeps" intended to draw the enemy from his bases. There were also alarms that led to swift departures and pursuits and in turn brought with them an increasing sense of anti-climax and frustration. For many years before, as it had grown in strength to remain the world's greatest fleet, the Royal Navy had been trained in the belief that a conflict with Germany was inevitable. Its spirit had been refined to a keen degree of belligerence and self-confidence in its own skill and weapons. The spirit of Nelson still burned. The nation was equally confident and expectant of a great and annihilating battle in the North Sea against this upstart sea power without a maritime tradition to its name. The Heligoland Bight affair occurred as a suitable prelude. When the main German fleet did not appear all through that winter, and its swift battle cruisers made cruel and humiliating tip-and-run raids against British east coast towns—only once were they caught but even then got away almost unscathed—it proved increasingly difficult for those in command up at Scapa Flow to prevent the fleet from succumbing to a sense of failure and inadequacy. What were they doing, they might have asked themselves, while the British army was bleeding to death in Belgium?

The ships of the Grand Fleet were, in fact, taking part in a distant blockade of Germany as effectively as Nelson's "far distant, storm-beaten ships, upon which the Grand Army never looked"* had blockaded France in the Napoleonic wars. But while Nelson's sailors were at sea and busily engaged in dealing with those storms, the men of the Grand Fleet were mostly at anchor, in the bleakest situation in the British Isles, with a good deal of time on their hands. What is more, in the new enlightened age, something less brutal than the whip of Nelson's day was required to sustain their fighting spirit. The means of achieving this end varied from ship to ship, and were nowhere more contrasting than between the two ex-Turkish battleships, the *Erin* (ex-*Reshadieh*) and *Agincourt,* which were anchored alongside one another. The Captain of the *Erin,* Lord Derby's brother the Hon. Victor Stanley, took little interest in the day-to-day running of his ship, which was properly in the hands of his Commander, Reggie Henderson. Henderson was marvellously efficient, and a first-class organizer. He was also

* *The Influence of Sea Power upon the French Revolution and Empire* by A. T. Mahan (1892).

adored by the whole ship's company. No ship coaled or shot or drilled or signalled more efficiently. She was also a "chatty" ship, a term that suggested carelessness both in appearance and cleanliness. "His ship's company", wrote a lieutenant from the *Agincourt,* "would do anything for Reggie Henderson, and his organization was superb, but as long as they drilled well, shot well, coaled ship well, he didn't mind what they or their ship looked like."

This policy conflicted directly with that of the Captain and the Commander of the *Agincourt,* and led to difficult relations between the two ex-Turkish battleships. On a bitter winter's morning, long before dawn in this bleak anchorage, the *Agincourt's* company would be called at 5.40 a.m. and had fallen in by 6 o'clock. They had been scrubbing or holystoning their ship's upper deck to a gleaming white for more than an hour when they heard from across the dark, windtorn waters of Scapa the *Erin's* crew being turned out of their hammocks. This sort of thing strained discipline beyond endurance and, on one occasion, resulted in the quarterdeck men of the *Agincourt* throwing overboard their holy-stones. Like the failure of the Board of Admiralty to protect the Grand Fleet's base against submarine attack, this human situation was one that had never been predicted in all the years of planning towards the inevitable Armageddon—that expected brief, bloody, glorious conflict in the North Sea.

Very few people in high places had envisaged a prolonged war of attrition, on land or at sea. Least of all had anyone—even the prescient "Jackie" Fisher—imagined that the spirit and fighting efficiency of the tens of thousands of men manning Britain's first line of defense would depend on the existence of football pitches and a ship with a large enough hold to put on concert parties. Such was the self-confidence of Britain at the height of her Imperial glory that, when war began, bases were undefended, new battleship construction was deferred (what was the use of laying down battleships in war-time if they would not be finished until two years after victory?). The idea of 35,000 men languishing in a state of boredom all through a long winter was beyond all contemplation. "The boys'll be home for Christmas"—that was the popular cry. No system of furlough was considered for more than a year from the outbreak of war.

However, by the early spring of 1915 steps were being taken to provide recreation and entertainment for the men at Scapa. Stone piers were built on the north side of the island of Flotta, and then working parties were landed to lay out football pitches for the men and a golf course for the officers. Later a wooden beer canteen was erected on the island, and the Church of Scotland replied with a Church Hut serving tea and buns. Cross-country running, pulling and sailing regattas between the ships, a primitive form of shooting and fishing for the officers, and (on board ship), deck hockey, medicine ball, deck golf, and high-cockalorum (an ancient, energetic, and often violent Royal Navy sporting activity) were among the activities which helped to fill in the time between regular shipboard duties and the occasional exercises at sea. Inter-ship competitions were the most popular and morale-sustaining. The *Erin* and *Agincourt* were arch-rivals, especially at tug-of-war and sailing, but this rivalry helped to seal the bond of friendship again between the two crews, and an afternoon of deck sports was usually followed by a guest night in which there was much consumption of gin and beer.

Concert parties became increasingly popular as this war of inaction continued. "The Agincourtiers" was drawn mainly from the cast of the Royal Yacht *Victoria and Albert* and had been especially popular with Queen Mary, who loved a borderline joke in the days of peace. Later, a stage was built in one of the two permanent frozen meat ships at Scapa, and this vessel would go alongside the ship giving a play or concert to offer better facilities and a larger auditorium. Several of the *Agincourt*'s officers were keen animal lovers, and live white ferrets (for digging out rabbits from their burrows on Flotta) and several dogs were kept on board, the ferrets being kept in a special cage on the after superstructure. The dogs roamed the ship at will except during practice firing, when they were confined, for their own comfort, to the 6-inch gun ammunition passages deep in the bowels of the ship.

By the spring of 1916 a well-established shipboard routine of drill, exercises, and entertainment had been established among the ships of the Grand Fleet. After nearly two years of war the officers and men of the *Agincourt* had conditioned their minds to an acceptance of the dismal fact that the German fleet did not want to fight, unless the odds were so strongly in their favor that they must win, a situation that could only occur due to some gross ineptitude on the part of Admiral Jellicoe. Too often the urgent summons to the North Sea, and to action stations, had resulted in a fruitless pursuit of a mythical enemy, and the disappointment of returning to the bleak northern anchorage. Britannia might still rule the waves, but while the fleet remained confined to Scapa Flow, it seemed an unexciting way of doing so.

Unknown to all but a handful of senior officers, a period of greater and more aggressive activity for both sides was imminent. It had never been the intention of the German C-in-C to confront the Grand Fleet in its full strength. Instead, from the earliest days it was hoped to nibble away at the superior power of the Royal Navy by overwhelming detachments of its scouting craft—light cruisers and Vice-Admiral Sir David Beatty's battle cruisers—with a superior force, and by making every effort to pick off individual battle ships by mines and the submarines' torpedoes. There had been an early success with the sinking by mine of the new British super-Dreadnought *Audacious* off the coast of Ireland. This had occurred at a time when the superiority of the Grand Fleet over the High Seas Fleet was at its lowest, owing to the detachment by the British Admiralty of strong forces of battle cruisers in search of Vice-Admiral Count Maximilian von Spee's cruiser force, which had all but extinguished British trade in the south Pacific. By early 1915 the strength of the British fleet had grown as new battleships laid down in 1912 and 1913 were completed and commissioned. In reply, Germany put her trust increasingly in the submarine to counter the British blockade. In 1915, 748,000 tons of British shipping went to the bottom as a result of U-boat attacks. "Unrestricted" U-boat warfare came to an abrupt halt when three American citizens were lost aboard the liner *Arabic*, which was sunk without warning, causing Washington to protest sharply. The campaign was renewed with fresh vigor in February, 1916, only to be brought to a halt when more Americans were killed in the steamer *Sussex* and Washington sent an ultimatum demanding from the German government "an abandonment of its present methods of submarine warfare against passenger and freight-carrying vessels" or face a break in diplomatic relations.

The month of February had also witnessed the appointment of a new, more skillful and aggressive German C-in-C, Admiral Reinhard Scheer. It was his intention to increase efforts to tempt out inferior British forces from their bases, cut them off and destroy them. His special target was Beatty's Battle Cruiser Force. This consisted of nine heavy ships, five of which were old and highly vulnerable, and all of them greatly inferior in defensive strength to the German battle cruisers. If Scheer could contrive to draw this force far enough away from the main British battle fleet, into the guns of his own battleships, and destroy even a part of them, he could upset the balance of power in the North Sea, and deliver a stunning blow to British morale. Over the next months Scheer devised and tried out unsuccessfully various methods of bringing this about. There were forays into the North Sea, but no contact between capital ships.

On the British side, Admiral Jellicoe ("the one man who could lose the war in an afternoon" as Churchill described him) was also being pressed by the Board of Admiralty to conduct a more aggressive policy, if only to offset some of the press and public criticism of the passive role of the well-named but disappointing Grand Fleet. For both sides, the diversion of public attention from the hell of Verdun was necessary, and only a victory at sea—a clean, quick, morale-raising victory—could provide this. Consequently, the German and British conduct of the war at sea became more daring, the offensive sweeps across the North Sea more intimidating and wider-ranging, until the laws of probability suggested that some time in May or June 1916 there would be a mighty meeting of the Dreadnoughts in the North Sea, if only by accident.

Of course there had been, since August 1914, a deep desire among the officers and men of the Royal Navy to come to grips with the enemy, and deep disappointment when every sweep into the North Sea resulted, it seemed inevitably, in a 16-point (180-degree) turn back to base without catching a glimpse even of the advanced scouting units of the High Seas Fleet. Nonetheless, the spirit of the Grand Fleet, and the High Seas Fleet too, had for long been conditioned to cautiousness and a concern for preserving *matériel*. The officers and men were innocent victims of the propaganda machines —from the officially supported Navy Leagues to the popular press—which for twenty years had been building up a sense of proud and admiring wonder in the ever more complex, ever bigger and more destructive weapons of war with which the fleets were being equipped. This Dreadnought enthusiasm, which had resulted in the doubling and tripling of the size and power of the German and British battle fleets (the broadside weight of a battleship's shells had risen 400 percent in less than ten years), had side effects of an entirely unpredictable nature. So vast, so expensive, so vital to the protective and destructive power of the fleet was each of these behemoths that their preservation became a dominant preoccupation of those who commanded them. In the days of sail, one could more easily flee from the enemy, so that, for example, high speed was considered an advantage in a frigate for this purpose as well as for catching the enemy. No one had thought of protecting a sailing man-of-war with special armour, but when the high explosive shell was developed and wrought iron was secured to the hulls of warships, a subtle change began to take place in the attitude of the fighting sailor. In the last half of the nineteenth century, with the introduction of even greater guns and the refinement of the mine and torpedo and submarine, naval architects were forced to give still more of their attention to the protection of their vessels, which because they were larger and more expensive were therefore less numerous. In the Russo-Japanese War Admiral Togo lost by mining two of his first-line battleships—one-third of his total force—in one day. By 1914 the descendants of Nelson's line-of-battle ships were costing around $12m. They took more than three years to build. Their hardened steel armour more than a foot thick, their elaborate honeycomb compartmentation (to reduce flooding), their batteries of quick-firing light guns to beat off torpedo-boat attack, the booms along their sides from stem to stern from which steel nets were suspended to halt and harmlessly explode the deadly torpedoes of the enemy, and even a portentous anti-aircraft gun or two indicated the great emphasis attached to their defense. What captain could look from his bridge onto this intricate and wonderful mass of machinery and ordnance, this product of ingenuity and taxpayers' sacrifice, without feeling intensely how much *had been entrusted to his care?* And what C-in-C could gaze out over Scapa Flow or the Jade without feeling an appalling weight of responsibility for the *preservation* of his armada? It was fear of destruction by mine and torpedo which had caused the British to withdraw their proposed close blockade of the German coast to a position based on the Royal Navy's northern bases, leaving the close blockade to light coastal forces. This had not only greatly reduced the chances of contact between the two fleets but also the range of operation of the Dreadnoughts which themselves were dependent for protective screening on short-endurance destroyers.

One other important factor must be added to those which

resulted in the cautious frame of mind and conduct of the
Grand Fleet since the beginning of the war. For more than
a century there had been little need for the British to study
war at sea seriously. Their supremacy had been almost un-
questioned, their arrogance amply justified. With the coming
of new *matériel* considerations in the early years of the century—the turbine, the stereoscopic rangefinder, director firing, the 15-inch gun, the small-tube boiler, and above all, the
epochal *Dreadnought* herself—the minds of the members of
the Board of Admiralty (and from them, down through all
echelons) became preoccupied with the need not only to
protect but also to understand and then to operate efficiently
the new weapons and machines which the age of technology
had offered to them. To many officers, brought up in the
days of spar and sail, this new era of science was awe-inspiring. Furthermore there was little time left over to study and
understand the real meaning and application of this appalling new power. Tactics were scarcely considered, and when
they were it was in terms of 1805. When war came, Jellicoe
rushed into print with the hastily-conceived Grand Fleet
Battle Orders. Jellicoe himself was trained in the traditions
of Fisher's suzerainty; he was, in fact, his protégé. The
C-in-C commanded without question, and individual initiative (it might lose the British a ship) was discouraged in
every one of the seventy close-printed sheets of the Battle
Orders. This was to be sea warfare with undisputed central-
ized command. And while it was desirable to seek out and
destroy the enemy, survival was all, "because our Fleet was
the one and only factor that was vital to the existence of the
Empire."

   It is a fine tribute to the spirit of the British sailor that, in
spite of this officially inspired policy of caution, the outcome
of a contest with the enemy was never seriously argued. The
self-confidence inspired by a century and a half of world
maritime dominance could not be suppressed so easily: the
doctrine of "We've got the ships, we've got the men, we've

got the money too!" did not die quickly. What was more, it was thought that the *matériel* was necessarily superior to the enemy's, for Royal Navy Dreadnoughts looked more battle-worthy and carried more and heavier guns.

The enemy was well aware of all this. The achievement of developing the German navy from a small coastal defense force to the second in the world in less than two decades was prodigious. But because the Germans had no sea-going tradition, they had none of the advantages of inherited superiority which sustained the British service. The German navy was superbly built, superbly trained, brilliantly officered, but from the beginning of the war it suffered from a sense of inferiority, nourished by statistical imbalance and a tactical policy governed by the need to avoid the enemy, unless he happened to be heavily outnumbered.

In April and May 1916, the clever and eager Scheer had set several Zeppelin and submarine traps to lure on to superior German forces Beatty's battle cruisers, which were normally stationed 200 miles south of Scapa Flow at Rosyth in the Forth estuary. Jellicoe busied himself with counter-plans governed by similar tactical motives. On May 15 Scheer tried again, deploying more than twenty of his submarines to form a net across the expected course of Beatty's scouting force and Jellicoe's supporting battle fleet when they were tempted from their bases by a diversion off the south Norwegian coast. This, too, failed. Jellicoe set June 2 as the date for springing another and more daring counter-trap. He was forestalled by Scheer. At one o'clock on the morning of May 31 Admiral Franz von Hipper ("Baby-killer" Hipper the British called him for his bombardments of east coast towns) sailed under cover of darkness from the estuary of the River Jade with his five battle cruisers and supporting light craft to create a diversion off the Danish coast. He was followed ninety minutes later, from the Jade and the Elbe, by the full might of Scheer's battle fleet, consisting of 22 battleships, all but six of post-Dreadnought design. This great force, itself almost twice as powerful as the entire United States Navy, steamed north through the small hours, Scheer stationing himself sixty miles behind his scouting force. Once again, German U-boats had been sent out earlier to report British counter movements and to torpedo some of the Dreadnoughts to reduce the British superiority in numbers.

British Intelligence had prior knowledge of these moves. The Germans were notoriously careless in their use of the radio. Moreover, the British had broken the enemy code early in the war, with the help of their Allies, the Russians, who had sunk a German cruiser in the Baltic and retrieved its code book and charts. More than twelve hours before Hipper set sail, Jellicoe had been informed by the Admiralty in London that there were indications of important German activity in the North Sea. At 5.40 p.m. on May 30, he was ordered to take the Grand Fleet to sea and concentrate a hundred miles east of the Scottish coast. "Be ready for any eventualities," he was warned.

At 6 o'clock in this northern latitude with mid-summer so near, there remained many hours of daylight. A flutter of flags hoisted from Jellicoe's flagship *Iron Duke* gave the "Preparatory signal for leaving harbour," followed by the time when the leading ship must pass through Hoxa Sound. This was followed in the *Agincourt,* as well as all her cohorts, by a brief period of intense activity. Men ashore on Flotta were urgently recalled, and down in the engine rooms steam had to be raised for the maximum cruising speed of 19 knots. Soon after 10 o'clock the whole of the Scapa Flow force had prepared for sea, raised anchors, and, beneath a vast pall of black smoke from hundreds of funnels, had slipped in predetermined order through the anti-submarine booms and out into the Pentland Firth and the open sea. It was a spectacle of powerful grace and magnificence. From the Scottish base of Cromarty there sailed the battleships of the 2nd Battle Squadron and the doomed squadron of old armoured cruisers commanded by the brilliant and fiery Rear-Admiral Sir Robert Keith Arbuthnot. Formed up in their cruising order of six columns in divisions in line ahead, columns disposed on either beam, the force, spread over a vast area of ocean, consisted of 22 Dreadnought battleships, supported by the scouting force of three battle cruisers led by Rear-Admiral the Hon. Sir Horace Hood.

But even this did not complete the armada. Simultaneously with his C-in-C's departure from Scapa Flow, Admiral Sir David Beatty with his flag in the battle cruiser *Lion* had cleared the Firth of Forth with five more battle cruisers, and the four battleships of the Fifth Battle Squadron. This last was the most formidable single fighting squadron in any navy. The *Queen Elizabeth* class of battleship was the very last word in naval design, possessing a speed close to that of the fastest battle cruiser, but also armour plate thick enough to resist the most powerful shell, and guns of 15-inch calibre, the largest in the world.

By brilliant organization, staff and intelligence work, this massive British armada was at sea, steaming towards the unknowing enemy before the German force had even cleared its home bases. If only Scheer would at last offer the chance of contact, everything pointed to the massive victory the Grand Fleet had been awaiting for almost two years.

In the *Agincourt* there was a feeling of relief among the ship's company in being at sea again, but little expectation of battle. Enthusiasm for combat was as high as ever, but numerous abortive sweeps through two winters and a summer had in turn dissolved any consciousness of crisis on these occasions. It was a clear, warm night with a touch of closeness in the air, and the steel gray seas through which the Grand Fleet advanced at an easy cruising pace of 15 knots were so smooth that only the faint vibration of the battleship's turbines and the wash of water against her hull told of movement. Darkness had scarcely closed about the ship before, at 3.30 a.m., the first light of dawn touched the horizon ahead. The orders were now to steam in search of enemy activity towards a rendezvous with Beatty's battle cruiser force off the Skagerrak at 2 o'clock on the following after-noon.

Any lingering hopes that the *Agincourt* might soon be firing her great guns at the enemy were dashed soon after mid-day on May 31 when Jellicoe received a telegram in-forming him that the German flagship—Admiral Scheer's *Friedrich der Grosse*—had not after all left the Jade. Neither side, then, knew that the other was out; while in fact and quite unknowingly the German and British fleets were for the first time, with their scouting forces positioned some two hours' sailing time in the van, steaming across the North Sea on courses which if maintained must result in the first meet-ing in modern history between two great Dreadnought fleets.

This curious state of affairs was brought about by several causes, all traceable in part to the fact that neither side had learned how to use efficiently their new instruments for com-munication and reconnaisance. Radar was still more than twenty years away and scouting by air was still primitive, yet it was only confusion in the interpretation of intercepted German radio signals that caused the Operations Division of the British Admiralty to pass on to Jellicoe the false news that Scheer was still in harbor when his battle fleet was actu-ally more than a hundred miles up the Danish coast. The British seaplane carrier *Compania* was left behind because her commander had never received the signal to sail from Scapa. It was a measure of the importance attached to the new-fangled air scouting that her absence was not noticed. Scheer for his part left his Zeppelins at home because he thought the weather was too bad for them to operate suc-cessfully.

For Jellicoe, the receipt of this false information was the first of several blunders committed by the Operations Divi-sion of the British Admiralty in London, and contributed to the haze of uncertainty which bedeviled him throughout the contest, just as the treacherous North Sea summer swathes of mist rose and fell unpredictably to obscure and reveal friend and foe alike. It came as a complete surprise to Jellicoe, then, when two hours after he had been informed that the enemy had not yet stirred from his base, his radio room took in a signal from Beatty's light cruiser *Galatea* sixty-five miles to the south: "Enemy in sight."

The *Agincourt* was the fourth and last ship in line in the extreme starboard column of the battle fleet. She was in the Sixth Division of the 1st Battle Squadron, under the flag of Vice-Admiral Sir Cecil Burney, Jellicoe's second-in-command, the three Dreadnoughts ahead of her being the *Marlborough* (flag), *Revenge* and *Hercules,* a heterogenous division with guns of 12-, 13.5-, and 15-inch calibre. Soon after 2.40 p.m. she acknowledged the signal to be ready for full speed, and then successively to cease zig-zagging (a protective measure against submarine attack) and increase speed to 17, then 18, knots. At 3 o'clock the signal was hoisted ordering complete readiness for action. The order had already filtered to every compartment in the ship, from the turrets where the gun crews had been at the ready since the previous night, to the stokers in the boiler rooms far below decks. As the guard rails were hastily cleared and the rigging frapped there was no attempt to conceal the sense of expectation and excitement among the officers and men. Hoses were run out on the upper deck (in battle they would be turned on as a fire precaution). Below decks, bedding and hammocks were struck down, and all stools and tables and other inflammable furniture hastily stored away from the risk of a fire. Another practical precaution was to put extra stoppers in the anchor cables in case a hit caused them to run out, and several more white ensigns were hoisted at the mast and yards in case her flag should be shot away. Ready-use ammunition for the ship's numerous 3-inch and 6-inch guns was got up from the magazines, and in the 12-inch turrets the crews took up their positions. Among the 1200 officers and men there was little anxiety about the notorious vulnerability of their great Dreadnought; dominating all other emotions was the throbbing excitement of expectation that

"The Gin Palace" was at last to prove her worth as the most heavily gunned warship in the world. At 18 knots she was vibrating heavily, and the beat of her engines could be heard even up on the bridge. Through the turret periscopes there could be seen a mile away the next column consisting of the early Dreadnoughts, *Colossus, Collingwood, Neptune,* and *St. Vincent,* all throwing up fine white bow waves; black smoke streamed from their eight funnels, met and multiplied, and fell astern in a rising, billowing cloud that seemed as if it would never disperse in the hazy afternoon sky. A mile beyond was another column, and then another, scarcely discernible, while the rest of the great armada was lost in the haze and its own funnel smoke.

At 3.45 p.m. the *Agincourt's* wireless room intercepted a signal to the flagship informing Jellicoe that Beatty's battle cruisers had sighted enemy ships to the north-east. The battle fleet had already altered course to south-east by south; now speed was increased to the maximum 20 knots as a further signal from Beatty carried the ringing message that he was engaging the enemy. It was the last message for almost one hour, a silence of agonizing suspense during which every officer and man above decks searched the horizon ahead for the first sight of gun flashes on the horizon, and listened for the deep thunder of distant guns.

At 4.45 p.m. the British battle fleet was still steering south-east by south at 20 knots, screened on both sides by the destroyer flotillas, and some twelve miles ahead by light and heavy cruisers, while farther ahead still and to the east of his C-in-C's line of advance was Admiral Hood's scouting force of three old battle cruisers, two of which, the *Inflexible* and *Indomitable,* had failed to catch the *Goeben* nearly two years earlier, but now rejuvenated were holding their maximum speed of 25 knots. Two minutes later, at 4.47 p.m., a W/T rating in the *Agincourt's* radio room picked up a stirring signal from one of Beatty's scouting cruisers far to the south east: "Have sighted enemy battle fleet . . ." So the whole High Seas Fleet was at sea! The message was piped so that the ship's company, from the sweating stokers far below to the shell handlers in the turrets, were appraised of the message for which they had been waiting for so long. Every officer and man stood and cheered.

This brief celebration, repeated in every unit of Jellicoe's battle fleet, would have been more restrained if the signal had included news of the disasters which had already overtaken the British battle cruisers during the previous hour since contact had been made between Beatty and the enemy.

The battle cruiser forces of Hipper and Beatty had made visual contact at 3.20 p.m. They were some fourteen miles apart. Hipper, flying his flag in the brand new battle cruiser *Lützow,* had four more heavy vessels all mounting 11-inch or 12-inch guns. Beatty, in the *Lion,* possessed a superiority of six to five in battle cruisers; but in addition as distant support some ten miles away he could also draw on the immense strength of Rear-Admiral Hugh Evan-Thomas's four fast 15-inch-gunned battleships, *Barham* (flag), *Malaya, Valiant* and *Warspite.* Beatty, in the belief that the main German battle fleet was still in port—had not the Admiralty confirmed this only a few hours earlier?—was determined to overwhelm his old antagonist who had escaped his clutches so often in the past. Hipper's task was to fight Beatty and at the same time draw him onto the guns of Scheer's great fleet hurrying northwards to close the trap. For the first time since the war had begun, both commanders were spoiling for a fight. Both commanders, too, were confident of annihilating the other. Neither believed that the main fleet of the other was at sea.

The first guns opened fire at 3.48 p.m., and at once a fierce running battle developed at a range of nine miles and at a speed of some 25 knots. The British were slow to get the range; the Germans, with the advantage of seeing their foe against a bright western sky, were remarkably quick, and drew first blood with a hit on the British flagship. Worse was to follow. A salvo of three 11-inch shells on the *Indefatigable* followed at once by more direct hits, caused this ship to blow up in two great explosions and disappear in a cloud of black smoke. Only two of her company of 1019 survived. Twenty minutes later the same fearful fate overtook the *Queen Mary*. On the bridge of his flagship, itself gravely wounded, Beatty turned to his Flag-Captain, remarked, "There seems to be something wrong with our bloody ships today," and ordered course to be altered to close the enemy. In this fierce contest little damage had been done to the enemy, while odds had swung to five to four in his favour.

But relief was at last on the way. Evan-Thomas had been struggling to catch up and bring his great ships into the battle. His 15-inch guns spoke at more than ten miles range at targets that could be only dimly and intermittently seen. Soon they were hitting, and when they did so causing fearful damage. But this running battle, now confused by smoke from funnels, guns and burning wreckage, by ever more variable visibility, and the sharp destroyer engagements between the lines, was fast approaching the German battle fleet, itself hastening north to complete the destruction of the British force. Visual contact was made at 4.30 p.m., offering Beatty the unexpected and momentous opportunity of reversing his rôle with that of his opponent, and in his turn drawing the whole German High Seas Fleet into Jellicoe's trap some sixty miles to the north-west.

At 4.40 p.m. Beatty ordered his surviving battle cruisers and battleships to turn 16 points (180 degrees) to starboard. There then began the second phase of the engagement, "the run to the north," during which for some one hundred minutes intermittent fire was exchanged between Beatty's battle cruisers and Evan-Thomas's battleships on the one hand, and Hipper's ships as well as the leading units of Scheer's battle fleet following close behind them. Evan-Thomas, now to the rear of his commander, took the brunt of the punishment, but also meted it out in good measure with his 15-inch guns, severely battering Hipper's tiring battle cruisers.

Admiral Jellicoe had been ill-served with information not only about the progress of the battle towards which he was hastening, but also on the whereabouts and course of both friend and foe. Soon after 5.30 p.m. he knew that a meeting was inevitable and imminent, and that he must soon make the critical decision on the most advantageous deployment of his fleet from cruising to battle formation. At 5.33 visual contact was made between Beatty's advance scouting cruiser the *Falmouth* and his own armoured cruiser *Black Prince,* and twenty minutes later Beatty, again heavily engaged with Hipper, caught the first glimpse of Jellicoe's leading battleships, bearing down from the north. He at once turned onto an easterly course in order to "bend" his opponent away from Jellicoe and delay Hipper's moment of recognition of the deadly trap into which he was leading his own C-in-C.

Through the periscope of number four ("Wednesday") turret in the *Agincourt,* the Lieutenant caught sight of the three wide-spaced funnels of Beatty's battered flagship, followed in line ahead by the *Princess Royal, Tiger* and *New Zealand,* all that was left of the First and Second Battle Cruiser Squadrons. The flashes of their 12-inch and 13.5-inch guns stabbed out in succession, and the proximity of the enemy was revealed by near-continuous orange ripples studding the horizon and the mast-high waterspouts from the shells straddling the British ships. More distant and to the south-west of the embroiled battle cruisers it was possible to pick out, dimly through the mist and smoke, Evan-Thomas's flagship *Barham* and the other units of his squadron, all as heavily engaged with an unseen foe.

A full-scale encounter could not be long delayed, and those on the bridge of the *Agincourt* waited anxiously for the signal to deploy as they searched the gun-flash scarred horizon for more tangible evidence of the enemy. Heavy shells were already falling between the columns of battleships from unseen guns when the signal was hoisted ordering the battle fleet to deploy to port, and at once the battleship *King George V* leading the extreme port column began to turn.

In quick succession the other leaders followed through ninety degrees. Shells were falling all about the *Agincourt*'s flagship *Marlborough* as she swung her helm over. At 20 knots it took less than a minute before the *Revenge* reached this same point ("Windy Corner" as it was to become known for the attention the German gunnery paid to this point of deployment for the Sixth Division battleships) and followed her flagship onto the new course. The *Hercules* was next, heeling hard over. Then it was the turn of the *Agincourt,* a vast target—"a bloody floating magazine" as they had called her. The shell spouts were rising all round her like the deadly grotesque blowing of gargantuan whales as her helm went over. Under more peaceful circumstances, this was always a tricky moment for the *Agincourt*. Such was her length and poor turning circle that she always had difficulty in matching the radius of turn of the rest of her division. Any failure to do so now would be especially disagreeable with the enemy apparently so near and getting the range so nicely.

The Navigating Officer conning the ship carried out the turn perfectly. But no one could ever explain how the *Agincourt* remained unscathed. As the last ship of the last division to deploy through "Windy Corner" she was nearer the van of the High Seas Fleet, those "great shapes looming up in an interminable line from the south," than any other battleship. For the same reason, she was the first to sight the leading German Dreadnoughts—the *König, Grosser Kurfürst, Kronprinz Wilhelm,* the *Markgraf* and the rest, though none was identifiable by name in the confusion of combat and the appalling visibility.

By 6.40 p.m. the deployment was complete, from six columns to the single classic line of battle, and the entire fleet, with the head already back onto a south-easterly course, was formed into a slight concave, a six-miles long trap of steel and ordnance; to Scheer the curved line was like the gates of hell as he came storming up from the south to complete the destruction of Beatty, only to be confronted instead by the entire Grand Fleet. It was the situation which he and his predecessors had strived to avoid since the beginning of the war. Deceived by Beatty's cunning and the uncertain visibility, failed by his scouting light cruisers, the German C-in-C's numerical odds had with dramatic suddenness changed from 27 to 8 in his favor to 35 to 27 against him. Moreover, his "T" had been crossed, the most dreaded ambush into which a naval commander could fall. Total destruction appeared inevitable.

As the heavy German ships came into sight, singly or in small groups out of the smoke and mist, the British battle fleet opened up. In this mêlée, with cruisers and destroyers "amidst this perfect deluge of shells . . . twisting and turning, endeavouring to avoid each other and the big ships"* there was no question of Jellicoe using distribution of fire signals; it was every ship for itself, as opportunity occurred. In the *Agincourt*'s turrets where tension was becoming almost unbearable as the thunder of battle increased, the relative bearing on which to train was awaited from the control top. The pointer on the Evershed bearing indicator in each turret began to swing. It steadied toward the center as the trainer closed in on the correct bearing. From the control top and the fore and aft bridges the seven turrets were seen to turn on their axes, to hesitate, then to settle on their bearing, while their fourteen guns fingered the sky hesitantly like the rifles of ponderous but well-drilled giant guardsmen, before steadying on a uniform elevation. Five miles away, seen only fitfully between swathes of smoke and mist and the spouts of bursting shells, was a battle cruiser—probably Hipper's *Lützow*.

In the *Agincourt*'s turrets they could hear above the crash of artillery the loud "Ting" of the fire gong—once, twice— then instantly the roar of the explosion. The guns recoiled. Breeches opened. The heady stink of cordite. Each new shell slid forward from the cage, the full four charges in their silk bags following. The "churn levers" were working per-

* *The Fighting at Jutland* by H. W. Fawcett and G. W. W. Hooper (1921).

fectly. The elevation and deflection were adjusted, the gongs rang out—and again the great crash. Then smoke from a friendly cruiser momentarily cut off the target. The battle cruiser reappeared, closer now, and fire was renewed, more furiously than ever.

These were full broadsides that the *Agincourt* was firing. Each time her structure shuddered under the immense recoil impact. But she withstood it all with massive unconcern; and "the sheet of flame," as one eyewitness in a nearby ship commented later, "was big enough to create the impression that a battle cruiser had blown up; it was awe-inspiring." If she survived the battle, "The Gin Palace" could never again be mocked for the supposed weakness of her ostentatious size and length.

But far ahead in the line another British battle cruiser *had* blown up. The *Invincible,* Admiral Hood's flagship, had also been shooting with great effect at the *Lützow.* Then three more enemy battle cruisers and a battleship got this old British battle cruiser—the first ever of her type—in their sights. She was hit several times. A shell drove through one of her midships turrets and exploded within, sending the armoured roof of the turret high into the air and exploding the cordite charges awaiting use far below. There were several terrible explosions, the ship broke exactly in half. When the *Agincourt* came rushing past, still firing, the *Invincible*'s two halves, already resting on the sea bed, stood up out of the water like twin gravestones beneath the smoke pall of her shroud. There had been other disasters, too. The British armoured cruisers, bent on self-immolation it seemed to all who saw them charge the German van, had taken a terrible beating. Their flagship *Defence* had blown up without a survivor, and another of their number was mortally wounded.

But the Germans, too, were suffering fearfully, especially the cruisers and battle cruisers. Hipper's flagship, *Lützow,* hauled out of the line at 6.37, her bows deep in the water, and was to sink later after the Admiral had transferred to his least damaged ship. Every gun in the *von der Tann* was out of action. The *Seydlitz* was awash up to the middle deck. The *Derfflinger* was scarcely able to fire, and she was taking in water from a huge hole in her bows.

The range was closing right down, and in spite of the ever-increasing smoke and failing light, the end of the German High Seas Fleet appeared near unless chance or supreme skill saved it. Already the line had been broken. Scheer acted desperately, ordering his destroyers into the attack at point-blank range and simultaneously hoisting the signal for the *Gefechtskehrtwendung,* or the battle about-turn, simultaneously ship by ship. Under any circumstances in close formation, there was a risk of collision. Under intense fire, in poor visibility, with formation already partly lost, it was an extreme measure justified only by the critical position in which the German C-in-C found himself.

The manoeuvre took from 6.33 to 6.45 p.m., and was accomplished with brilliant skill and without accident. No one in the *Agincourt,* nor even Jellicoe himself, recognized what was happening. So short had been the glimpses of the High Seas Fleet, that its total absence passed without notice for several minutes. Furthermore the German destroyer attack was a successful diversion. The 12-inch gun crews in the *Agincourt* were awaiting a target, and there had been a brief pause in the cacophony of sound, when the entire starboard battery of ten six-inch guns opened up. Everyone thought the ship had been hit. Then a glance through the turret periscopes showed the German destroyers coming in, and being straddled again and again. Two were seen to be hit by the *Agincourt* as the Schwartzkopf torpedoes whistled from their tubes, dived into the sea and sped towards the British line. From the *Agincourt's* bridge, by their line of tell-tale bubbles, they could be seen coming, and the helm was put hard over. Three were evaded, and a fourth was soon to stop in the water and surface just short of the ship. The Division's flagship was less fortunate, and soon the *Marlborough* could be seen heeling over as the sea came pouring in.

The destroyers, too, disappeared into the mist and smoke, and a lull fell over the battle fleet. Course was altered to south-east, and then to south in an effort to cut off Scheer from his bases. The German C-in-C recognised this danger all too clearly, and soon after he was clear of the enemy's heavy artillery, he reversed course again in an effort to get behind the Grand Fleet. It was another highly dangerous decision to take, and demanded most skilful timing and exact information on the whereabouts of the enemy. Scheer failed on the first count, and was misinformed on the second. Soon after seven o'clock, the entire High Seas Fleet, now ragged in its formation and gravely damaged in the van, came blundering back into the jaws of Jellicoe.

The British could scarcely credit their good fortune. The light had improved again, the mist dispersed, and the smoke of battle had diminished since the first conflict. At 7.15 p.m. the German battle cruisers and the leading Division of battleships appeared magically, and clearly, in the sights of the entire fleet at ranges varying from six to twelve miles.

From the control top of the *Agincourt* one of the *Kaiser* class battleships was selected, and fire opened at 11,000 yards. Once again the heavy ordnance blasted out, and between salvoes as news of hits was given to the sweating gun crews the men cheered. In number four turret the periscope glass misted over from the fumes from the gun blasts and spray from the enemy's near misses, and the range-taker climbed out of the turret to clean it. Soon after, the range began to increase, the rate of opening becoming 750 yards a minute. At 15,000 yards the *Agincourt* lost sight of her target, and the fire died down. Again the German destroyers were coming in, firing their tubes and laying smoke.

The German C-in-C had acted again with promptitude and daring in an effort to correct his second appalling error. Within three minutes of sighting the British gun flashes (the light was now against him and he could see no more), he signalled his battered and almost impotent battle cruisers: *"Schlachtrkeuzer ran an den Feind, voll einsetzen"* (Battle cruisers, charge the enemy with everything you have), an order that was to become as famous as any in naval history, and one which resulted in Hipper's famous "death ride." Then he sent in his flotillas, ordering them to attack at close range and make smoke to conceal his next movement, which was to repeat the earlier *Gefechtskehrtwendung*. Although almost all semblance of order in the High Seas Fleet had now been lost, communications were as excellent as before, and so was the carrying out of this difficult evolution. Each British ship in turn lost sight of its target, and the range widened still further when Jellicoe ordered a cautious turn-away from the enemy's torpedoes.

Although neither side could have believed it possible at the time, the Battle of Jutland was concluded with that final retreat of the German Fleet behind its own black smoke screen soon after 7.20 p.m. on the evening of May 31st. The British had never been trained to fight a major night engage-ment—the risks, it was considered, were too high—but in the *Agincourt,* as in every British Dreadnought, expectation was high that the enemy would be caught at dawn before it reached harbour. All through that mid-summer night there were fierce brief engagements between the light forces of the two fleets, and an old German battleship was blown up by a torpedo. From the *Agincourt* the flash of gunfire occa-sionally lit the horizon, and once the shape of a large ship was seen to pass down the starboard side and to disappear within seconds as silently as it had come. It was only one of a number of unexplained contacts, whether between friend and foe or friend and friend will never be known, which occurred during those dark hours when the two fleets groped their way about blindly and hazardously off the coast of Denmark.

At first light of day the *Agincourt*'s division found itself alone on a calm, sunny, slightly misty sea. The injuries to the flagship *Marlborough* had so reduced their speed that all contact with the C-in-C had been lost, and Admiral Burney shifted his flag to the *Revenge* and set about trying to regain the Division's station. Their course took them across the scene of the meeting between the two fleets, and all about them they saw the debris of ammunition cases, lifebelts, the wreckage and litter of all kinds and the inevitable patches of oil which in their melancholy confusion are the aftermath of any great combat at sea. Far away above the horizon there hung in still and silver splendour the long tubular shape of a German Zeppelin, on the prowl, scouting for information. It was far beyond the range of the *Agincourt*'s single little anti-aircraft gun; but as a gesture it was manned and fired. Then, before it slid out of sight, the *Revenge* raised its 15-inch guns to maximum elevation and fired a defiant salvo. It was said later that her shells caused consternation among Evan-Thomas's battleships out of sight some fifteen miles away.

The *Marlborough,* no longer battle-worthy, was detached and sent back under escort to the nearest British base. The other surviving Dreadnoughts of the Division searched fruit-lessly for their C-in-C; and then as the warm, sunny day wore on, slowly reconciled themselves to the fact that the battle was over, and set course for Scapa Flow. "Our excitement at having taken part in a major fleet action evaporated slowly," one of the *Agincourt*'s lieutenants remembers. As the elation diminished, a thorough examination of the ship for damage was conducted. "The Gin Palace" had been for-tunate. The near-misses of shells and torpedoes had been numerous, and all that could be found, besides the destruc-tion of the remaining old Turkish-inscribed crockery, was splinter damage from a heavy shell on the after superstruc-ture. By unhappy chance, a single splinter had broken open the wooden hutch where the five white ferrets were kept. They were nowhere to be found. Several weeks passed before they were discovered, black with coal dust, in a bunker deep down in the bowels of the ship. They had survived, it seemed, on a diet of rats.

The *Agincourt*'s war was over when she anchored again in Scapa Flow on June 2, 1916. Although he had suffered less than his adversaries, Scheer never again risked a fleet action with the Royal Navy, and the Germans turned more and more to submarine warfare—a policy which came near to starving out Britain but resulted finally in the entry of the United States into the European war. Like the rest of the battle fleet, the *Agincourt* experienced no more combat, and saw the German fleet again only on that impressive occasion in the North Sea on November 21st, 1918, for its surrender to Admiral Sir David Beatty, who had succeeded Jellicoe after Jutland. The war years had brought about few changes to the battleship. She was still the most comfortable and spacious ship in the Royal Navy, or in any navy. In 1918 she was little altered in outward appearance, too, although more anti-aircraft guns now broke up the vast area of her quarter deck, and betokened a new age of maritime warfare that would one day spell the doom of even the greatest battle ship. There were, too, now more searchlights, her after superstructure had been built up higher, her main tripod mast had gone, its absence adding further to her impression of fleet pugnaciousness. The years of war had brought along battleships of greater tonnage. But still nothing could match her splendour, and still no battleship carried as many heavy guns—a distinction she was to hold for all time.

After the war the Admiralty still regarded the *Agincourt* with a jaundiced eye—as a bastard not of their creating, as a monster misfit with no useful role to play now that the emergency circumstances were finished. Early in 1919 she was packed off into the Reserve while a buyer was sought. And who would want this great ship now? The Admiralty thought that the Brazilians might like her after all, now that their economic situation was sounder as a result of the war. The Ministry of Marine in Rio de Janeiro turned her down after some consideration. The Turkish fleet was already in Allied hands, and that ruled out her other previous owner. So she was brought back to Armstrongs where she was to be modernized by conversion to oil fuel and by the addition of much more protection. This, it was thought, might make her a more saleable proposition. But no one was interested, not now. The renovations were halted, and for a time she was used—and this was surely the ultimate humiliation—by the Royal Navy for experimental purposes, like some offering to the vivisectionists. From this she was mercifully saved in 1922, to be sent off to the breaker's yard instead. And by the end of the year the blow torches had torn her asunder.

No warship in the whole Grand Fleet was better loved by those who served in her. Those who survive today remember her with warmth, and the proprietary pride of a child for its Great Dane. For many of her company she was a home for more than four years of war. So powerful was this affection that one feels, had she been mined or torpedoed, or badly struck by German shell, her weaknesses would have been overcome, and by faith alone she might somehow have been kept afloat. Perhaps it is some measure of the real greatness of this ship that the fears and the jealousies she aroused during her long period of construction were matched by the deep loyalty felt for her by those who were eventually destined to serve in her.

INDEX

THE GREAT DREADNOUGHT

The Strange Story of
H.M.S. Agincourt

by Richard Hough

Few ships have been so awesome in
their might or so curious in their
history as was H.M.S. *Agincourt*. In
the period of violent nationalism and
fierce naval rivalries that preceded
World War I, she was the ultimate sea-
going weapon, the battleship of battleships. Born of an arms-race in one
hemisphere, she became a focus of intrigue half a world away, and took
part in the greatest naval battle of
World War I.

The largest fighting ship afloat,
she could hurl nearly 12,000 pounds of
high explosives at the enemy every
thirty seconds. This book tells her fas-
cinating story. It is a story of mutiny,
financial and political machinations
and international intrigue. Even as
her giant guns were being mounted
and her splendid furnishings readied,
ownership of the vessel passed from